A DICTIONARY OF
⊨ LATIN WORDS AND PHRASES ⊨

━━◄OPTIMIS PARENTIBUS►━━

A DICTIONARY OF

LATIN WORDS AND PHRASES

JAMES MORWOOD

Oxford   New York

OXFORD UNIVERSITY PRESS

1998

Oxford University Press, Great Clarendon Street, Oxford OX2 6DP

Oxford New York

Athens Auckland Bangkok Bogota Bombay Buenos Aires
Calcutta Cape Town Dar es Salaam Delhi Florence Hong Kong Istanbul
Karachi Kuala Lumpur Madras Madrid Melbourne Mexico City
Nairobi Paris Singapore Taipei Tokyo Toronto Warsaw

and associated companies in
Berlin Ibadan

Oxford is a trade mark of Oxford University Press

Published in the United States
by Oxford University Press Inc., New York

British Library Cataloguing in Publication Data
Data available

Library of Congress Cataloging in Publication Data
Data available
ISBN 0–19–860109–3 (Pbk.)

1 3 5 7 9 10 8 6 4 2

Typeset by Alliance Phototypesetters
Printed in Great Britain
on acid-free paper by
Mackays of Chatham
Chatham, Kent

⇥ CONTENTS ⇤

⇒+ PREFACE +⇐

A DICTIONARY OF THIS KIND will owe much to many
sources. Of the valuable Oxford books I have used, I should
like to single out *The Concise Oxford Dictionary of Proverbs* by
John Simpson (Oxford, 1992), *The Concise Oxford Companion to Classical Literature* by Margaret Howatson and Ian Chilvers (Oxford,
1993), and *The Little Oxford Dictionary of Quotations*, edited by Susan
Ratcliffe (Oxford, 1994) to whose selection of themes my topic-
based index owes almost everything. My greatest debt is to *The
Oxford English Dictionary* and to its staff (especially Edmund
Weiner). I, of course, must take full responsibility for any short-
comings in the use I have made of this help.

Moving out from Oxford, I am delighted to acknowledge my
debt to *The World of Rome*, edited by Peter Jones and Keith Sidwell
(Cambridge, 1997), and to the Packard Humanities Institute's CD-
Rom PHI which contains the corpus of Latin literature (including
the Vulgate) and has enabled me to track down many quotations
and give them their references—as well as unmasking a few
impostors which had crept into the line-up. The aims of recent
tillers of the same field as myself have been very different from
mine, but I must express my debt to Eugene Ehrlich, whose *Dictionary of Latin Tags and Phrases* (London, 1987) is sprightly and
avuncular in tone, and to Klaus Bartels and Ludwig Huber, whose
small book *Veni, Vidi, Vici* (Zurich, 1966), written in German, is a
splendid encapsulation of the *multum in parvo* principle.

I must express my gratitude to colleagues in the Literae
Humaniores faculty at Oxford (especially Don Fowler), and at
Wadham College, Oxford (especially Allan Chapman and Cliff
Davies). Sidney Allen, Ted Kenney, Ian McAuslan and Keith Rose
have given valuable advice. Jennifer Speake has made an important contibution as copy-editor. At Oxford University Press, Sarah
McNamee has proved an indefatigable factotum, and Susie Dent,
my publisher for this and other books, has been as helpful and
supportive as ever.

JAMES MORWOOD
Wadham College

⇥ INTRODUCTION ⇤

C HAUCER'S VILE SUMMONER starts to parrot Latin legal tags when drunk.[1] He has picked them up without understanding them during the considerable time he has spent in the ecclesiastical court, where Latin terms were used. He would have benefited from a dictionary of this kind. Latin was a fundamental part of English communication in the Middle Ages, and it still is. Its tenacity is remarkable. On 6 September 1995, most British newspapers carried a story about civil servants in the Treasury abandoning Latin tags because today's breed of its employees could make nothing of them. On 17 September the *Sunday Telegraph* launched a wildly successful fifteen-week Latin course called *QED: Learn Latin by Christmas.*[2]

Latin gave its alphabet to England and to the Western world generally. In England, it was the language of the Christian Church until the Reformation, and was used internationally in the worship of Roman Catholics into the 1960s. Until the Renaissance had passed, it was the language of international communication. Until the seventeenth century, it was the language of the Western world's science. Isaac Newton published his *Principia Mathematica* (The Principles of Mathematics) in Latin in 1687, and as late as 1716 Edmund Halley chose Latin for his forecast of a transit of Venus that was going to take place forty-five years later. This was still the way to gain the widest international audience. Doctors used to write out prescriptions in Latin. The language was vital for government and business and thus fundamental to the curriculum of the many grammar schools set up in the sixteenth and seventeenth centuries. The statutes of Oundle School in Northamptonshire (founded in 1556) demand that all boys should converse in Latin to each other 'as well in the school as coming and going to and from the same'. It was the language of utility as well as respect.

---

[1] The General Prologue to the *Canterbury Tales*, 639–48.
[2] This course has now been published in book form as *QED* by Peter Jones (Duckworth, 1997).

Thus, until recently, all our greatest politicians and men of literature were taught Latin. The language became a means by which the educated would show off their learning to mutual admiration. Such displays of combined quickness and erudition—when, for example, a speaker in the House of Commons could extract in a trice from his mental computer the absolutely appropriate Latin expression for the occasion—were a significant characteristic of a privileged coterie. Those days are dead, and that kind of display can now seem self-congratulatory and self-indulgent. Even so, I hope that this dictionary will enable its users to savour something of that sense of sharing in a cultural experience which depends on an awareness that the Romans had a word for it long before we did. Women are now welcome as well as men! (The topic-based General Index should prove of especial help to those who wish to find a Latin expression for a particular context.) However, Latin has permeated the thoughts and the feelings of English-speakers in a far more profound way than mere witty exhibitionism. To see that, one has only to look at the index entries in this book under, say, *Joy and sorrow*, *Love*, and *Death*. This is scarcely surprising. After all, more than half the words in English come from Latin.

The entries in this dictionary vary in their nature. Many of them simply give an English translation of the Latin. When they are quotations from Latin literature, I have added a reference to where they come from, and, when it seems to me to be interesting and relevant, I have outlined the context. (The section on Latin writers (pp. 190–9) may prove to be of value here.) Where words and phrases are naturalized in English, I have taken from *The Oxford English Dictionary* their date of entry into published English and quoted their first published use if it is helpful. If not, I have quoted a later use with its date. References to quotations in all these examples are taken from *OED* and the curious should find it possible to track them down. I have not included most words which have been totally naturalized in English (e.g. focus, index, media) since they have long ceased to be Latin and would be out of place here.

I have tried, probably not altogether successfully, to avoid the note of coyness and over-ingenuity that can afflict such a collection. Proverbs (see separate index) are restricted to those that are natural both in English and in Latin, and the mottoes in the General Index are almost all the well-known ones that have an application to life in general as well as the institutions or people who have adopted them. (Many more mottoes are to be found in the body of the dictionary.) Legal terms (see separate index) have been pared down very substantially, though a considerable number remain. Medical ones have been cut to the bone. The Christian emphasis in such a dictionary is inevitable, and for those who wish to pursue the relevant entries (see separate index on Christianity and the Church), recognition of the names of the books in the Bible and some knowledge of Christian worship are useful. I need hardly add that I have no intention of indicating a patronizing attitude to other religions.

Long syllables are marked in all the Latin entries. These, after a brief reading of the rules under 2 in the first section of the essay on *Pronunciation*, will enable users to speak the entries with the correct stress. The rest of the essay should prove helpful and, as I hope, interesting.

Entries are entirely alphabetical, for this purpose ignoring gaps between words (e.g. *invita Minerva* comes before *in vitro*). Some tags appear in more than one form; where it has seemed appropriate, I have written different entries to reflect the different wording. As can be inferred from above, in addition to the topic-based General Index, there are indexes on Christianity and the Church, the Law and Proverbs.

⇥ PRONUNCIATION ⇤

NUMBER OF SYLLABLES, AND STRESS IN LATIN

The following rules should always be observed:

1 Except in obvious diphthongs (*ae, au, oe,* often *eu*), every single vowel belongs to a syllable, as in the English word 'recipe' (three syllables). Thus in Latin *dēsine* is three syllables and *diem* is two.

2 The stress in Latin words of more than two syllables falls on the penultimate syllable if this is 'heavy' (i.e. has a 'long' vowel or a vowel before two consonants), e.g. *festína, agénda*. It falls on the antepenultimate (third from last) syllable when the penultimate syllable has a 'light' (a 'short') vowel, e.g. *dóminus*.

The stress falls on the first syllable of two-syllable words.

Everything recommended in **2** is natural for English speakers.

In the entries in this dictionary all vowels which are 'long' have been marked. A vowel before two consonants will be 'heavy' but not necessarily 'long'. All vowels which are unmarked or not before two consonants are 'light' ('short').

THE PRONUNCIATION OF CONSONANTS AND VOWELS

As far as the English pronunciation of the sayings and phrases in this dictionary is concerned, we must pick our way through a minefield. I begin with a guide to the pronunciation of classical Latin, which readers may choose to follow. The English sounds referred to are those of 'Oxford English', a Southern English dialect.

⇥ CONSONANTS

Consonants are pronounced as in modern English, but note the following:

c always hard, as in cat (never soft as in nice)*

g always hard, as in God (except when it is followed by **n**; **gn** is sounded **ngn** as in hangnail: so **magnus** is pronounced **mangnus**)*

h always sounded, as in hope

i used as a consonant as well as a vowel; as a consonant it sounds like English **y**; so Latin **iam** is pronounced **yam**

q never found except when followed by **u**, sounded as in English **quick**

r rolled as in Scottish, and always sounded (so in Latin **sors** both **r** and **s** are sounded)

s always soft, as in **sit** (never like **z**, as in rose)

v pronounced like English **w** (so **vīdī** sounds **weedee**)

Where double consonants occur, as in sitting, both consonants are pronounced; so **ille** is pronounced *ille* (l is sounded long).

✦ VOWELS

a short, as in English **cup** (not as in cap)
ā long, as in English **father**
e short, as in English **pet**
ē long, as in English **aim** (French **gai**)
i short, as in English **dip**
ī long, as in English **deep**
o short, as in English **pot**
ō long, as in English **foal** (French **beau**)
u short, as in English **put**
ū long, as in English **fool**

✦ DIPHTHONGS

A diphthong can be defined as a glide from one vowel to another within the same syllable.

ae as in English **high***
au as in English **how**
ei as in English **eight**
eu e-u
oe as in English **boy**
ui u-i

*In Church Latin (appropriate to the entries in the index Christianity and the Church), **c** and **g** before **e** and **i** are pronounced **ch** and **j**, **gn** is pronounced **ny**, and **ae** is pronounced **ay**. Overall an Italianate pronunciation should be adopted.

The above recommendations are based on W. Sidney Allen's *Vox Latina: A Guide to the Pronunciation of Classical Latin* (Cambridge,

1965, reprinted 1978, revised 1988). Sidney Allen was the Professor of Comparative Philology at Cambridge, and the compiler of this dictionary had the privilege of attending his lively and stimulating lectures on the pronunciation of Greek and Latin in the 1960s. His important philological work has ensured that English-speakers are now likely to pronounce Latin with greater accuracy than those who have been taught within any other tradition.

However, over the centuries, Latin has sounded very different indeed from what is recommended here. As Allen remarks, 'anyone who has listened to Latin as pronounced until recently in the Westminster play, or at Grace by elder members of Oxford and Cambridge high tables, or in legal phraseology, will be aware that it bears little relation to the pronunciation with which we have been concerned' (*Vox Latina*, p. 102).

Users of this dictionary may therefore find it helpful to read the following brief account (strongly indebted to Allen (*Vox Latina*, pp. 102–10); see also L. P. Wilkinson, *Golden Latin Artistry* (Cambridge, 1963), pp. 3–6) of the pronunciation of Latin in England.

THE PRONUNCIATION OF LATIN IN ENGLAND

Throughout the centuries in which Latin has been spoken in England, native speech habits have had a considerable effect. In the Old English period there was no attempt to observe the correct vowel lengths except in the penultimate syllables of words of more than two syllables: thus *mínimīs* and *melióra*. The first syllable of a two-syllable word was rendered 'heavy' by lengthening the first vowel if it was originally 'light' (e.g. *lībrum* for *librum*). Also s after vowels was pronounced as z.

After the Norman conquest, the French influence made itself strongly felt. Consonantal i and g (before vowels) were pronounced j (e.g. in *iūstum* and *genus*), c (before vowels) was pronounced s (so *Cicerō* became *Siserō*, as he remains in English to this day), and long vowels before two or more consonants were pronounced short (*nūllus* becoming *nullus*). The tendency to lengthen short vowels was reinforced (e.g. *tēnet* and *fōcus* for *tenet* and *focus*).

In the mid fourteenth century English started to establish itself as the medium for the teaching of Latin in England, which had its effect on the pronunciation of the language. Then in 1528

Erasmus' dialogue *De recta Latini Graecique sermonis pronunctiatione* (Concerning the correct pronunciation of Latin and Greek) was published in Basle. This light-hearted conversation between a bear (the instructor) and a lion was a milestone on the journey towards the re-establishment of the classical pronunciation. It recommends *inter alia* hard c and g before all vowels and the pronunciation of s as simply s where a z sound had become traditional (e.g. in *mīlitēs*). In addition, it reasserts the importance of vowel length.

While Erasmus does not appear to have actually used his reformed pronunciation, his work had an important if gradual influence. Attempts to establish his recommended pronunciation at Cambridge, however, were temporarily halted when the chancellor of the university published in 1542 an edict specifically forbidding it. Undergraduates, he claimed, were becoming insolent in making use of an 'exotic' pronunciation and relishing the fact that their elders could not understand it.

The chancellor's edict was repealed in 1558. Even so, the new pronunciation was obstructed by inertia and the prejudice of traditionalists as well as by developments in English as the Middle English vowel system shifted to modern English. These meant that the Latin vowels a, i and e were pronounced as in English *name*, *wine* and *seen*. In addition, in words of more than two syllables with a 'light' penultimate, the antepenultimate (stressed) vowel was generally shortened. Thus *Oedipus* and *Aeschylus* became *Edipus* and *Eschylus*—as they remain in the USA—and *Caesaris* became *Cesaris*.

In the mid nineteenth century vowel length began to be correctly taught, and hard g and c were established in some quarters. However, around 1870 there came to a head a feeling that something far more radical had to be done about the chaos in the pronunciation of classical Latin, and by the end of the century all the responsible bodies in England representing schools, universities and learned societies had recommended the adoption of an authentic scheme of pronunciation formulated by various Cambridge and Oxford colleges.

However, inertia as well as downright opposition ensured that the reforms took at least a generation to come into effect. Especially controversial was the recognition that in Latin there is no letter v (the consonantal u is correct). Thus *vēnī*, *vīdī*, *vīcī* should be pronounced *wayny*, *weedy*, *weaky*—which struck some as being very funny. So late was this particular development that in most of the sayings and phrases and in the Anglicized words (such as *vīvā*) in this dictionary, authenticity in the tradition of English practice should lead to the use of the v sound.

Even as late as 1939 *The Times* received—and suppressed—a letter against the old pronunciation by the Kennedy Professor of Latin at Cambridge, and the controversy lingered on until the 1950s. In addition, it has to be acknowledged that, as Allen crisply remarks, the reforms 'do not go so far as to involve any actually non-English sounds' (*Vox Latina*, p. 106). In fact it has been Allen's work, enthusiastically propagated by the Joint Association of Classical Teachers, which has eventually shifted the English pronunciation of classical Latin closer to the Mediterranean basin.

CONCLUSION

This brief history of the sound of Latin in English can be taken as a licence that, in the pronunciation of the entries in this dictionary, more or less anything goes. Certainly it is only recently that they have stood any chance of receiving an authentic classical pronunciation from English-speakers. The compiler thus welcomes his readers to a Babel of conflicting and mainly ersatz Latinate sounds.

⤞THE DICTIONARY A–Z⤝

NOTE: For the rules relating to where the stress falls in Latin words, see 2 of the first section of the essay on Pronunciation on p. x.

ab aeternō
> ~ from the beginning of time.

ab asinō lānam
> ~ literally, 'wool from an ass', i.e. blood from a stone.

Used of an attempt at the impossible.

ā bene placitō
> ~ at pleasure, at one's will.

abeunt studia in mōrēs
> ~ '(one's) pursuits/hobbies "come out" in (one's) character', i.e. our personalities are shaped by our enthusiasms.

OVID *Heroides* xv.83.

ab extrā
> ~ from outside.

First recorded use in English 1642.

1864 MRS GASKELL *Wives and Daughters* 1.ix.101 It was a great relief to her to have Mr. Gibson to decide for her . . . Such decisions *ab extra*, are sometimes a wonderful relief.

ab honestō virum bonum nihil dēterret
> ~ nothing deters a good man from acting honourably.

Based on SENECA *Letters* lxxvi.18.

abiit, excessit, ēvāsit, ērūpit
> ~ he has gone, he has left, he has got away, he has broken out.

CICERO *In Catilinam* II.i.1. Cicero delivered his first speech against Catiline, whom he accused of conspiracy against the Roman republic, before the Senate on 8 November 63 BC. Later that day Catiline fled from Rome. In these words from near the start of his second speech, delivered on the following day, Cicero forcefully conveys the precipitate speed of Catiline's flight.

ab īmō pectore

~ from the bottom of the heart, i.e. with deep and sincere emotion.

Based on CATULLUS lxiv.198, LUCRETIUS *De Rerum Natura* iii.57, and VIRGIL *Aeneid* i.371, 485.

ab incūnābulīs

~ from the cradle, i.e from infancy.

ab initiō

~ from the beginning.

1600 B. JONSON *Every Man out of his Humour* Prologue If those laws . . . had been delivered us *ab initio* and in their present virtue and perfection.

Also used as an adjective.

1943 T. HORSLEY *Find, Fix & Strike* 21 The Swordfish was used as an *ab-initio* trainer.

ab intestātō

~ from an intestate person.

Used with reference to a succession, inheritance, etc.

1785 T. JEFFERSON *Papers* (1953) VIII.191 The citizens or subjects of each party shall have the power to dispose of their personal goods within the jurisdiction of the other by testament, donation or otherwise: and their representatives, *whosoever they be*, shall succeed to their said personal goods whether by testament or ab intestato.

ab intrā

~ from within.

1672 T. JACOMB *Romans* v.186 When 'tis [sc. sin] committed with little opposition *ab intra*, and in spight of all opposition *ab extra*, I assure you then it hath a great power.

ab orīgine

~ from the origin.

Derivation of the word 'aborigine', applied to one thought to be an inhabitant of a country 'ab origine'.

ab ovō

~ from the egg, i.e. from the (very) beginning.

HORACE *Satires* I.iii.6 (see next entry) and *Art of Poetry* 147.

Alternatively, the phrase may refer to a passage in Stasinos' epic poem the *Little Iliad*, in which he begins his account of the Trojan War with the egg of Leda from which Helen was born. If Leda had not laid this egg, Helen would not have been born. If Helen had not been born, Paris could not have run off with her. If Paris had not run off with Helen, the Trojan War would not have taken place, etc. Thus it was an egg that started it all.

1586 P. SIDNEY *Apology for Poetry* (1595) sig. K1v If they [dramatic poets] will represent an history, they must not (as *Horace* saith) begin *ab ovo*: but they must come to the principal point of that one action, which they will represent.

ab ovō usque ad māla
~ literally, 'from the egg to the apples' (in a Roman banquet), i.e. from the beginning to the end.

HORACE *Satires* I.iii.6. a Roman dinner would start with eggs and end with fruit.

absēns haerēs nōn erit
~ literally, 'the absent person will not be the heir', i.e. out of sight, out of mind.

absente reō
~ in the absence of the defendant.

absit
~ let him/her be absent, i.e. permission given to a student to be absent.

1884 C. DICKENS *Dictionary of the University of Cambridge* 3/1 *Absit*, every Undergraduate wishing to leave Cambridge for a whole day, whether including a night or not, must obtain an 'absit' from his Tutor.

absit invidia
~ literally, 'let ill feeling be absent', i.e. no offence intended.

absit ōmen
~ 'let there be no (ill) omen', as, for example, in the word or words one has just used.

First recorded use in English 1594.

1886 *Athenaeum* 20 Feb. 260/1 He says that if the Queen herself were to shoot Mr. Gladstone through the head (*absit omen!*) no court in England could take cognizance of the act.

ab ūnō disce omnēs

∼ from one man learn about all (of the Greeks), i.e. from one example you can learn what the whole of a group is like.

VIRGIL *Aeneid* ii.65–6. Virgil's hero Aeneas describes the plausible acting of a Greek agent called Sinon whose trickery led the Trojans to take the wooden horse into Troy and thus caused the city's destruction. From Sinon's trickery, says Aeneas, you can learn a lesson about all the Greeks.

ab urbe conditā (AUC)

∼ from the foundation of the city (of Rome).

The traditional date of the founding of Rome by Romulus was 753 BC.

1761 L. STERNE *Tristram Shandy* III.xxxvi.167 'Tis just as discreditable and unscholar-like a question, Sir, as to have asked what year (*ab urb. con.*) the second Punic war broke out.

1979 C. JAMES *Flying Visits* 76 About the time the city of Rome was being founded—the year zero *ab urbe condita*.

abūsus nōn tollit ūsum

∼ abuse does not do away with use, i.e. that something can be abused is no reason for putting an end to its legitimate use.

abyssus abyssum invocat

∼ literally, 'abyss calls to abyss', i.e. one depravity leads to another.

ā capite ad calcem

∼ from head to heel, i.e. thoroughly, through and through.

acceptissima semper mūnera sunt, auctor quae pretiōsa facit

∼ those gifts which the giver makes precious are always most welcome.

OVID *Heroides* xvii.71. Helen does not reject the gifts of Paris. Cf. Shakespeare, *Hamlet* III.i.101: 'Rich gifts wax poor when givers prove unkind.'

accipere quam facere iniūriam praestat

∼ it is better to receive an injury than to inflict one.

Based on CICERO *Tusculan Disputations* v.56.

accūsāre nēmō sē dēbet

∼ no one is bound to incriminate himself.

Acherontis pābulum
~ literally, 'food for Acheron' (one of the rivers of the classical hell).

PLAUTUS *Casina* II.i.12. This expression, spoken of her husband by a discontented wife, is a wish for a bad man's death and subsequent illtreatment (i.e. being devoured) in the underworld.

a cruce salūs
~ from the cross (comes) salvation, i.e. the death of Christ on the cross and his subsequent resurrection lead to salvation for Christians.

ācta est fābula
~ the play is finished, i.e. it's all over.

A Latin version of some Greek words which were among the last spoken by the first Roman emperor Augustus (SUETONIUS *Augustus* xcix.1). The last words of Rabelais were 'La farce est jouée', and Leoncavallo's opera *I Pagliacci* ends with the line 'La commedia è finita'.

āctum est dē rēpūblicā
~ it is all over with the republic.

āctum nē agās
~ literally, 'do not do what is already done', i.e. once something is settled, it's settled.

A saying quoted by TERENCE *Phormio* II.iii.72.

āctus reus
~ guilty act: the action or conduct which constitutes a crime, as opposed to the mental state of the accused *see* MENS REA.

1902 C. S. KENNY *Outlines of Criminal Law* iii.44 In these cases, from the difficulty of obtaining legal evidence of the offender's knowledge of one portion of his *actus reus* (*e.g.*, the adulteration, or the drunkenness), something much less than actual knowledge is allowed to suffice in respect of that portion.

ā cuspide corōna
~ 'a crown from (gained by) the spear', i.e. by gallant fighting.

ad absurdum
~ literally, 'to the point of absurdity', denoting an argument, statement, etc. which draws on or demonstrates a ridiculous conclusion.

1734 G. BERKELEY *Analyst* para. 25.41 Why any other apagogical Demonstration, or Demonstration *ad absurdum* should be admitted.

ad arbitrium
∼ at will, at pleasure.

ad astra
∼ to the stars, i.e. to an elevated state.

ad astra per ardua
∼ to the stars through difficulties, i.e. greatness is only achieved by surmounting problems.

This is the motto of the State of Kansas, USA.

ad captandum (vulgus)
∼ (calculated) to take the fancy of (the crowd).

1762 T. SMOLLETT *Launcelot Greaves* l.x.201 These paltry tricks, *ad captandum vulgus*, can have no effect but on idiots.

ad Calendās Graecās
See AD KALENDAS GRAECAS

ad crumēnam
∼ to the purse, i.e. appealing to financial considerations.

addendum (plural addenda)
∼ a thing to be added; an appendix or addition.

1794 R. BURNS *Works* IV.179 You cannot, in my opinion, dispense with a bass to your addenda airs.

1897 O. W. HOLMES *Motley* xxi.179 After I had gone over the instructions for the last time I wrote an addendum.

ā Deō et rēge
∼ from God and the king.

adeste fidēlēs
∼ o come, all ye faithful.

A Christian hymn written in Latin, sung at Christmas. The writer is unknown; the music is by John Reading.

ad extrēmum
∼ at last.

ad fēminam

~ literally, 'to a woman', applied to an argument or statement either directed against a woman or appealing to her interests.

1972 *Village Voice* (N.Y.) 1 June 80/2 Well mehitable how Are things down at pussy lib Headquarters here I am sorry to report The attack is ad feminam From our old friend Ed hoagland.

ad fīnem

~ to the end, i.e. towards the end, especially of a piece of writing.

Used in references.

ad hoc

~ for this purpose, to this end; for the particular purpose in hand or in view.

First recorded use in English 1659.

1875 W. R. GREG *Miscellaneous Essays* (1882) vi.147 A sum not far off two millions per annum will have to be provided *ad hoc* by the Chancellor of the Exchequer.

Used as adjective.

1955 *Times* 14 May 11/1 He was still employed by the B.B.C. on *ad hoc* basis as a programme producer.

Hence the nonce-words *adhoc(k)ing, ad hoc-ery, ad hocism, ad-hoc-ness*: e.g. *Economist* 14 Oct. 1961 124/1 Britain thrives on 'anomalies' and 'ad hoc-eries'.

ad hominem

~ to the (individual) man, i.e. relating to the principles or preferences of a particular person rather than to abstract truth or logical cogency.

First recorded use in English 1599.

1633 W. AMES *Fresh Suit* I.x.105 Some arguments, and answers are *ad hominem*, that is, they respect the thing in question, not simply, but as it commeth from such a man.

adhūc sub iūdice līs est

~ the dispute is still before the court.

HORACE *Ars Poetica* 78. Horace here says that scholars are still arguing about who invented the verse form, elegy; his Latin words can be more generally applied to any matter about which debate still continues. *See also* SUB IUDICE.

ad īnfīnītum

~ to an indefinite degree of extent, endlessly, for ever.

First recorded use in English 1678.

1733 J. SWIFT *On Poetry* in *Works* (1755) IV.1.194 A flea Hath smaller fleas that on him prey, And these have smaller still to bite 'em, And so proceed *ad infinitum*.

ad interim

~ in the mean time, during the interval.

1856 *Farmer's Magazine* Nov. 377 That *ad interim* the recommendations of the Lords Committee of 1851 would be acted upon.

ad Kalendās Graecās

~ literally, 'at the Greek Kalends', i.e. never.

The Greeks had no Kalends, the Roman name for the first of the month.

ad libitum (abbreviated to ad lib.)

~ at will, as much as one pleases.

First recorded use in English 1610.

1962 N. DEL MAR *R. Strauss* I.vi.183 He never gave them [saxophones] any solo work, marked them *ad lib.*, and ... omitted them in his own perform-ances.

ad-lib. (verb) to speak extempore, improvise.

First recorded use in English 1919.

1958 N. SHUTE *Rainbow & Rose* iii.95 The whole squadron in the stalls chi-hiking at us and Judy ad-libbing back at them across the footlights.

ad līmina (Apostolōrum)

~ literally, 'to the threshold (of the Apostles)'.

Originally used with reference to a pilgrimage made to the tombs of St Peter and St Paul in Rome; in later use, referring to the obligatory periodic visit of a Catholic bishop to the Holy See to report on the state of his dio-cese.

1900 A. S. BARNES *St. Peter in Rome* xiv.354 We have here ... an ornament pre-sented to the church by an emperor of the first half of the fifth century ... clearly visible to every pilgrim who comes to pay his visit *ad limina Apostolorum*.

1992 *Irish Times* 26 Sept. 11/1 These novel opinions ... in the context of the *ad limina* visit by the Irish hierarchy to Rome ... are loaded with political meaning.

ad locum (abbreviated to ad loc.)
~ at or to the place.

A reference to where a matter is discussed most fully in a book.

1829 *U. S. Circuit Court (1st Circuit) 'Mason' Reports* iv.92 See Laws Wisbuy, art. 24 ...; Cleirac ad Loc. p. 29.

ad maiōrem Deī glōriam (abbreviated to AMDG)
~ for the greater glory of God.

The motto of the Christian society of Jesuits, used especially as a dedicatory formula.

ad misericordiam
~ (an appeal or argument) to mercy or pity.

1824 *Edinburgh Review* XLI.55 The fallacy of those arguments *ad misericordiam* on which the agriculturists now principally rest their claims to protection.

ad nauseam
~ to the point of disgust or revulsion.

First recorded use in English 1616.

1955 *Bulletin of Atomic Scientists* Jan. 15/1 The cliché that fear is altogether and always uncreative is being repeated ad nauseam.

ad patrēs
~ (gathered) to the fathers, i.e. dead.

ad praesēns ova crās pullīs sunt meliōra
~ literally, 'eggs immediately available are better than chickens tomorrow', i.e. a bird in the hand is worth two in the bush.

ad rem
~ (pertaining or pertinent) to the matter or subject in hand, to the purpose.

1608 T. MIDDLETON *The Famelie of Love* v.H. 4 *Ad rem, ad rem*, master Poppin: leave your allegories, . . . and to the point.

Cf. AD HOMINEM.

1680 J. HOWE *Letter to Person of Quality* 23 What I can find in his Sermon hath any aspect or design that way is either *ad rem* or *ad hominem*.

adscrīptus glēbae
~ allocated (i.e. bound) to the soil.

Used of serfs.

adsum

~ 'I am here'.

Used as an answer in a roll-call.

ad unguem

~ literally, (fashioned) to the fingernail, to a nicety, i.e. without flaw.

HORACE *Satires* I.v.32–3. Horace uses this phrase of one Fonteius Capito, a man without a defect, a perfect gentleman. The fingernail belongs to the sculptor who would pass it over the marble to make sure that it was smooth.

ad ūnum omnēs

~ all to a man.

ad ūsum Delphīnī

~ literally, 'for the Dauphin's use', i.e. expurgated.

See IN USUM DELPHINI.

ad utrumque parātus

~ prepared for either event.

VIRGIL *Aeneid* ii.61–2. The reference is to the Greek agent Sinon who, in his successful attempt to persuade the Trojans to take the wooden horse into their city, was prepared either to win through with his trickery or to die.

advocātus diabolī

~ the 'devil's advocate', one who urges the devil's plea against the canonization of a saint, or in opposition to the honouring of anyone; hence, one who advocates the contrary or wrong side for the sake of argument, or injures a cause by his advocacy.

First recorded use in English 1842.

1929 *Music & Letters* X.194 It is a pleasant thing to play *advocatus diaboli* with the knowledge that one is going to allow oneself to cross over to the angels' bench later.

aegrēscit medendō

~ he she it grows worse by the remedy.

VIRGIL *Aeneid* xii.46. The Italian king Latinus tries to calm the rage of the young prince Turnus against the Trojan invader Aeneas, but his reasonable words merely serve to inflame Turnus' frenzy.

aegrōtat
~ he/she is sick.

At Oxford and Cambridge universities, a certificate that a student is too ill to attend an examination.

1864 C. BARBAGE *Philosopher* 37 I sent my servant to the apothecary for a thing called an aegrotat, which I understood . . . meant a certificate that I was indisposed.

aequam servāre mentem
~ to preserve an equable mind.

An abbreviation of *aequam memento rebus in arduis servare mentem* (remember to keep a calm mind in difficulties) (HORACE *Odes* II.iii.1). It was a traditional piece of wisdom that one should treat disaster and triumph with equal indifference.

aequō animō
~ with equal, i.e. equable mind.

Cf. English derivative 'equanimity'.

aere perennius
~ more enduring than bronze.

HORACE *Odes* III.xxx.1. He has built a monument more lasting than bronze—and indeed than the royal pyramids (l. 2)—in his poetry.

See ARS LONGA, BREVIS VITA.

aetātis suae
~ of his her age.

E.g. (on a tombstone) died aetatis suae 24.

See ANNO AETATIS SUAE.

ā fortiōrī
~ by a stronger reason, all the more.

First recorded use in English 1606.

1855 H. SPENCER *The principles of psychology* (1872) I.ii.i.146 The expression 'substance of Mind' can have no meaning ... *A fortiori*, the substance of Mind cannot be known.

ā fronte praecipitium, ā tergō lupī
~ literally, 'in front a fall from a great height, behind wolves', i.e. between the devil and the deep blue sea; it is hard or impossible to choose between the appalling alternatives.

agenda

∼ things to be done, matters needing attention, usually the items of business to be considered at a meeting.

1907 *N.U.T. Conference Agenda* (Oxford) 30 This Conference protests against the action of the Executive in printing Supplementary Agendas for Conference.

1982 *Scientific American* Sept. 45/2 The issue is once again high on the agenda of the West German trade unions.

age quod agis

∼ do what you do carefully; concentrate on the business in hand.

agnōscō veteris vestīgia flammae

∼ I recognize the return of the old fires (of love).

VIRGIL *Aeneid* iv.23. Dido finds that the love which she had felt for her murdered husband Sychaeus is reviving in her obsession with Aeneas.

Agnus Deī

∼ the Lamb of God. **a** a part of the Roman Catholic Mass beginning with the words *Agnus Dei, qui tollis peccata mundi* (O Lamb of God, that takest away the sins of the world); also the music set to it. **b** a figure of a lamb bearing a cross or flag. **c** a cake of wax or dough stamped with such a figure, blessed by the Pope and distributed by him on the Sunday after Easter.

albō lapillō notāre diem

∼ to mark the day with a white stone, to decide that it has been a happy day.

PLINY *Natural History* VII.xl.41. A reference to the Thracian custom of recording days as good with white or bad with black pebbles.

Alcinoō pōma dare

∼ to give fruit to Alcinous, i.e. to carry coals to Newcastle.

The wondrous garden of Alcinous, king of the Phaeacians, is described at length in HOMER *Odyssey* vii.112ff. To give him fruit would be a ridiculously superfluous action. *quis . . . poma det Alcinoo?* (who would give fruit to Alcinous?) is Ovid's adaptation of the proverb (*Ex Ponto* IV.ii.10).

ālea iacta est

∼ the die is cast.

SUETONIUS (*Julius Caesar* 32) tells how in 49 BC Julius Caesar debated whether to cross the Rubicon, the river which constituted the boundary between Gaul and Italy, with his legions. To do so would inevitably be to plunge the Roman world into civil war. With the exclamation *iacta alea est*, he went ahead. This is a gambler's metaphor: 'die' is the singular of 'dice'.

alere flammam
∼ to feed the flame.

alia tentanda via est
∼ another way must be tried.

aliās
∼ literally, 'otherwise', i.e. otherwise called.

First recorded use in English 1535.

1607 SHAKESPEARE *Coriolanus* II.i.48 Violent testy magistrates (alias fools).

As noun, meaning an assumed name.

1605 W. CAMDEN *Remains* (1614) 147 An *alias* or double name cannot prejudice the honest.

alibī
∼ literally, 'elsewhere', i.e. the plea of having been elsewhere at the time when any alleged act took place.

1743 H. FIELDING *Jonathan Wild* in *Miscellanies* III.IV.iii.303 A single *alibi* would have saved them.

aliēnī appetēns, suī profūsus
∼ eager for the possessions of others and lavish of his own.

SALLUST *Catiline* v.4. In a brilliant set piece, the historian sums up the complementary vices and virtues of the (in his view) essentially vicious Catiline.

aliquando bonus dormītat Homērus
∼ even good Homer sometimes nods.

HORACE *Ars Poetica* 359. Even the greatest of poets can be off form.

aliquid haeret
∼ something sticks.

alma māter
∼ literally, 'nurturing mother'.

Today used of one's college or university.

alter ego
~ my other self, a second self, a trusted friend.

1537 R. LAYTON *Let.* 4 June in *Lett. Suppress. Monast.* (1843) 156 You must have such as ye may trust even as well as your own self, which must be unto you as *alter ego.*

alter īdem
~ another self, i.e. a trusted friend.

See preceding entry.

alter ipse amīcus
~ a friend is another self.

alternātim
~ alternately: in church music, the performance of a work antiphonally, as by alternating sections of the choir, in different styles of singing, or by alternation of voices with organ or other instruments.

1958 *Listener* 2 Oct. 540/3 Among the Masses are straightfoward polyphonic works ... and there are the late Mantuan works intended for alternatim performance.

altissima quaeque flūmina minimō sonō lābī
~ literally, 'all the deepest rivers slip by with the least sound', i.e. still waters run deep.

alumnus (plural alumnī)
~ literally, 'nursling', i.e. a pupil of a school or university, a graduate or former student.

1645 J. EVELYN *Diary* (1827) 1.212 We saw an Italian comedy acted by their alumni before the Cardinals.

amābilis īnsānia
~ a pleasing madness or rapture.

HORACE *Odes* III.iv.5–6. Horace wonders whether others can hear the Muse, or is it a delightful delusion?

amantēs āmentēs
~ lovers (are) mad.

Based on PLAUTUS *Mercator* 81 and TERENCE *Andria* 218.

amantium īrae amōris integrātiō est
~ lovers' quarrels are a renewal of love.

TERENCE *Andria* III.iii.23.

amāre et sapēre vix deō concēditur

∼ to be in love and wise is scarce granted even to a god.

PUBLILIUS SYRUS *Sententiae* A.22.

amārī aliquid

∼ some touch of bitterness.

LUCRETIUS *De Rerum Natura* iv.1130.

See SURGIT AMARI ALIQUID.

ā maximīs ad minima

∼ from the greatest to the least, i.e. from things of great import to trivialities (referring to things or matters, not people).

ā mēnsā et t(h)orō

∼ from board and bed, a legal separation in English law before 1857.

First recorded use in English 1600. Thoro is an Anglicized spelling.

1683 J. OWEN *Sermons* (1721) 572 This divorce *a mensa & thoro* only is no true divorce, but a mere fiction of a divorce.

amīcī probantur rēbus adversīs

∼ friends are tested by adversity (while a fair-weather friend will abandon you when troubles come).

amīcus certus in rē incertā cernitur

∼ a sure friend is seen in an unsure situation; a friend in need is a friend in deed.

ENNIUS *Tragedies* 351, quoted by Cicero at *De Amicitia* xvii.64.

amīcus cūriae

∼ literally, 'friend of the court', i.e. a disinterested adviser.

First recorded use in English 1612.

1837 C. DICKENS *Pickwick Papers* x.95 I shall be happy to receive any private suggestions of yours, as *amicus curiae*.

amīcus Platō, amīcus Sōcratēs, sed magis amīca veritās

∼ Plato is dear to me, Socrates is dear, but truth is dearer still.

A very free Latin version of a phrase of Aristotle's in the *Nichomachean Ethics*: 'Where both are friends it is right to prefer truth'.

amīcus usque ad ārās

~ a friend as far as the altars, i.e. as far as is permitted without causing offence to the gods when friendship may come into conflict with religious beliefs.

amor nummī

~ love of money.

amor patriae

~ love of country, patriotism.

amor scelerātus habendī

~ the accursed love of possessing.

OVID (*Metamorphoses* i.131) talks of the early days of the world: first there was the golden age, then the silver, then the bronze. The age of hard iron came last, bringing evil to mankind. Ovid's phrase refers to the breakdown of the idealized communism of the early men.

anathēma sit

~ let him be accursed. **a** the great curse of the Church, cutting off a person from the communion of the Church and handing him or her over to Satan. **b** the denunciation of any doctrine or practice as damnable.

1 Corinthians 16.22.

anguis in herbā

~ snake in the grass.

VIRGIL *Eclogues* iii.93. A character in Virgil's poem warns some boys of the danger that lurks amid the flowers, strawberries and grass of a beautiful landscape. The expression thus counsels against putting too much trust in appearances.

anīlēs fābulae

~ old wives' tales.

Based on HORACE *Satires* II.vi.77–8.

anima nātūrāliter Christiāna

~ a soul naturally Christian, i.e. one who behaves like a Christian without the benefit of Christian revelation.

TERTULLIAN *Apologia* 17.

anima vagula

~ little soul flitting away.

The beginning of a poem ascribed to the dying emperor Hadrian and still to be read on the wall of his mausoleum (the Castel Sant'Angelo in Rome). It has been translated or paraphrased by Prior, Pope, Byron, and Dean Merivale.

animīs opibusque parātī
~ literally, 'prepared in spirit and resources', i.e. ready for anything.

annō aetātis suae
~ in the year of his age, the full version of AETATIS SUAE.

Annō Dominī (AD)
~ in the year of our Lord, in the Christian era.

Western calendars date the passage of time from the birth of Christ. The expression is also used jocularly of advanced or advancing age.

1885 F. GALE *The life of the Hon. Robert Grimston* xvi.284 Whenever he felt less able to do things than formerly, he used to say he was afraid 'Anno Domini' was the cause.

annō hegirae (AH)
~ in the year of the hegira, i.e. in the year of the flight (Arabic *hijirah* = Latin (and English) *hegira*) of Muhammad from Mecca to Medina.

This year (AD 622) is taken as the start of the Muslim era, and for Muslims the passage of time is thus dated from what Western calendars refer to as 16 July 622. The Muslim equivalent of AD 2000 is AH 1421.

annō mundī
~ in the year of the world.

Literal belief in the events of the Old Testament has led to some specific estimates as to when the world began. The Hebrew tradition puts this at what Western calendars call 3761 BC. In the seventeenth century an Irish theologian called Ussher calculated the date of creation to be 4004 BC; thus the *anno mundi* equivalent of AD 2000 is AM 6004.

annō urbis conditae (AUC)
~ in (such or such a) year (counted) from the founding of the city (of Rome), generally reckoned to be 753 BC.

See AB URBE CONDITA.

annuit coeptīs
~ he (God) has favoured our undertakings.

A motto on the reverse of the great seal of the United States of America, which is printed on the reverse of the $1 note. In the decidedly more aesthetic context of the original, VIRGIL (*Georgics* i.40) asks Augustus Caesar to favour his undertaking as he embarks on his poem about farming.

annus horribilis
~ a horrible year, i.e. a disastrous or particularly unpleasant year.

First recorded use in English 1985.

1992 QUEEN ELIZABETH II in *Times* 25 Nov. 3/2 1992 is not a year I shall look back on with undiluted pleasure. In the words of one of my more sympathetic correspondents, it has turned out to be an 'annus horribilis'.

annus mīrābilis
~ literally, 'a wonderful year', i.e. a remarkable or auspicious year.

1667 J. DRYDEN (title) Annus Mirabilis: the year of wonders, 1666 [in which the Great Fire ravaged London].

1959 *Listener* 13 Aug. 251/1 By then he [sc. Tennyson] was successful and famous, his *annus mirabilis* of 1850 already three years behind him.

ante
~ before, earlier in a book, passage, law, etc.

Used in cross-references, especially in legal texts.
First recorded use in English 1688.

1987 S. CALLIGAN *Points to Prove* 94 Examples of common contraventions of statutory provisions are shown at point 6 *ante*.

ante-bellum
~ before the war, especially, before the American Civil War (1861–5), the South African War (1899–1902) or either of the World Wars (1914–18 and 1939–45).

1862 M. B. CHESTNUT *Diary* 14 June (1905) 188 Her face was as placid and unmoved as in antebellum days.

ante merīdiem (a.m.)
~ before midday.

ante tubam trepidat
~ before the trumpet (for battle sounds), he trembles with fear.

Based on VIRGIL *Aeneid* xi.424.

apage Satanās
~ Get thee hence, Satan!

Greek version of RETRO ME, SATANE.

apologia prō vītā suā
~ a defence of his life.

The title of the religious autobiography (1864) of John Henry Newman, who converted from Anglicanism to Catholicism in 1845. There is also a reference to the *Apology* of Socrates, the philosopher's decidedly unapologetic speech in his defence in 399 BC as recorded by his pupil Plato; he had been accused of impiety and of corrupting the young.

ā posse ad esse
~ from possibility to actuality, i.e. making a possibility actually happen.

ā posteriōrī
~ literally, 'from what comes later', i.e. reasoning or arguing from that which follows, from effect to cause, from experience and not from axioms.

1624 F. WHITE *Replie to Fisher* sig. C4v Your other argument ... is, *a posteriori*, from an example of the ... French King, Henry the fourth, to whom you wish his Majesty to be a parallel.

Also used facetiously, meaning 'from behind', 'on the buttocks'.

1762 T. SMOLLETT *Launcelot Greaves* ix.200 One of them clapped a furze-bush under the tail of Gilbert, who, feeling himself thus stimulated *a posteriori*, kicked and plunged and capered.

apparātus bellī
~ materials of war.

apparātus criticus
~ a collection of palaeographical and critical matter accompanying an edition of a text.

1865 J. CONINGTON *Vergili Opera* l,p.x The publication of Ribbeck's *apparatus criticus* has made a new recension necessary.

ā priōrī
~ literally, 'from what is before', i.e. arguing from cause to effect.

First recorded use in English 1710.

1862 J. MCCOSH *Supernat.* II.i.2.132 Reason commands us, in matters of experience, to be guided by observational evidence, and not by *a priori* principles.

aquā et igne interdictus

∿ literally, 'forbidden water and fire', i.e. banished.

Water and fire are seen as symbolic of life within a community.

aquam ē pūmicī nunc postulās

∿ you want to get water from pumice stone, i.e. you are trying to get blood from a stone.

PLAUTUS *Persa* 41.

aqua rēgia

∿ a mixture of nitric and hydrochloric acids, so called because it can dissolve the 'noble' metals, gold and platinum.

1610 B. JONSON *Alchemist* II.v What's cohobation? 'Tis the pouring on Your *aqua regis*, and then drawing him off.

aqua vītae

∿ literally, 'water of life', an alchemist's term for pure alcohol.

Cf. 1471 G. RIPLEY *The compound of alchymy* in Ashmole 1652 p. 115 With Aquavite oft times, both wash and dry.

Also meaning strong liquor.

1547 A. BOORDE *A compendious regyment or a deyetary of helth* x.258 To speak of . . . aqua vite or of Ipocras.

aquila nōn capit muscās

∿ an eagle does not catch flies; superior to paltry considerations, the king of birds maintains his dignity.

arbiter bibendī

∿ toastmaster.

At a Roman banquet this person would take charge not only of the rate of drinking but also of the strength of the wine, which was regularly diluted.

arbiter ēlegantiae/ēlegantiārum

∿ literally, 'judge of elegance', i.e. a judge in matters of taste.

TACITUS *Annals* xvi.18. Said of Gaius Petronius, who was given the additional name (*cognomen*) Arbiter since he performed that function at the court of Nero.

Arcades ambō

∼ literally, 'both Arcadians', i.e. both (of them) pastoral poets or musicians (Arcadia being a supposedly idyllic pastoral location), thus persons of the same tastes, profession, or character (often derogatory).

The reference is to VIRGIL *Eclogues* vii.4, where the two Arcadians, Corydon and Thyrsis, engage in a poetry competition, which Corydon wins.

1821 BYRON *Don Juan* IV.xciii Each pull'd different ways with many an oath, 'Arcades ambo', *id est*—blackguards both.

arcāna imperiī

∼ literally, 'secrets of the empire', i.e. state secrets.

argūmentum ad crumēnam

∼ literally, 'an argument relating to the purse', i.e. an appeal based on financial considerations.

argumēntum ad hominem

∼ an argument directed towards the man (addressed), that is, founded on the principles, practices, or character of an opponent.

See AD HOMINEM.

argūmentum ad ignōrantiam

∼ an argument founded on the ignorance (of one's opponent).

argūmentum ad verēcundiam

∼ an argument appealing to feelings of decency.

arma virumque canō

∼ I sing of arms and the man.

In these opening words of his *Aeneid*, Virgil announces his intention to sing of Aeneas, the man who led the refugees from the sacked city of Troy to Italy where, after a bloody war, he carved out a foothold for them, thus enabling them to become the Romans of the future. *arma* (= arms) looks back to Homer's *Iliad*, the story of the fighting round Troy, and *virum* (= man) to his *Odyssey*, the first word of which is 'man' (i.e. Odysseus). George Bernard Shaw's play *Arms and the Man* is an ironical evocation of this highly charged heroic opening of the greatest Roman epic.

arrēctīs auribus

∼ literally, 'with ears erect', i.e. attentively.

VIRGIL *Aeneid* i.152 and ii.303 and SILIUS ITALICUS *Punica* x.458.

ars est cēlāre artem
> ∿ art consists in concealing art; when creative artistry proves truly successful, one does not notice the 'art' (skill) that has gone into the creative process.

ars grātiā artis
> ∿ art for art's sake.

The motto of Metro-Goldwyn-Mayer, the film-producers.

ars longa, vīta brevis
> ∿ art is long, life is short.

Based on SENECA *Dialogi* x.i.1. Seneca here translates the Greek of Hippocrates, who is referring to the art of healing.

artium baccalaureus
> ∿ Bachelor of Arts (BA), the undergraduate degree awarded by universities and colleges.

artium magister
> ∿ Master of Arts (MA), a higher university degree than BA.

asinus ad lyram
> ∿ the ass at the lyre.

VARRO, quoted in GELLIUS iii.16, from a Greek proverbial expression ὄνος πρὸς λύραν. The expression implies ludicrous unfitness for an undertaking, though Varro appears to be signifying untimeliness.

astra castra, nūmen lūmen
> ∿ the stars my camp, the Deity my lamp.

Athanasius contrā mundum
> ∿ Athanasius against the world, i.e. one resolute man facing universal opposition.

Athanasius was archbishop of Alexandria in the reign of the emperor Constantine, and author of the Athanasian Creed which begins with the words QUICUNQUE VULT.

at spēs nōn frācta
> ∿ but hope is not broken.

auctor pretiōsa facit
> ∿ the giver makes the gifts precious.

OVID *Heroides* xvii.71–2. Ovid imagines Helen replying to Paris' suggestion that she should run away with him. He has promised her enormously impressive gifts. She responds by saying that it is he rather than the gifts that she values: it is his love for her that renders them precious. *See* ACCEPTISSIMA SEMPER MUNERA SUNT, AUCTOR QUAE PRETIOSA FACIT.

audācēs fortūna iuvat

∿ fortune favours the bold.

A popular Latin tag. God helps him who helps himself. *See* AUDENTES FORTUNA IUVAT.

audentēs fortūna iuvat

∿ fortune favours the daring.

VIRGIL (*Aeneid* x.284) puts these proverbial Latin words into the mouth of Aeneas' Italian opponent, the prince Turnus. This is all that Virgil had written of this line (which, if completed, would have been more than twice as long) at his death and so it rings out with especial emphasis. The words are to backfire on Turnus, for the poem ends with his slaughter at the hands of Aeneas. *See* AUDACES FORTUNA IUVAT.

audē sapēre

∿ dare to know. Cf. SAPERE AUDE.

audī alteram partem

∿ hear the other side.

ST AUGUSTINE (*De Duabus Animabus* xiv.2) here insists that there are two sides to every question.

auditque vocātus Apollō

∿ and Apollo hears when invoked.

VIRGIL (*Georgics* iv.7) hopes that Apollo, god of poetry, will assist him in the final book of his poem about farming, in which he deals with bees. The expression means that the gods listen when called upon.

aura populāris

∿ the popular breeze, i.e. the veering to and fro of the people's favour.

Based on CICERO *De Haruspicum Responsis* xx.43.

aurea mediocritās

∿ the golden mean.

HORACE (*Odes* II.x.5) praises moderation, echoing a number of Greek writers. A famous Greek statement of this ideal was inscribed on the temple of Apollo at Delphi: μηδὲν ἄγαν (= nothing in excess). One should not aim to rise above a certain station in life, and one's approach to life should be moderate.

aureō hāmō piscārī
~ literally, 'to fish with a golden hook', i.e. the game is not worth the candle.

Based on SUETONIUS *Augustus* 25.

auribus teneō lupum
~ I am holding a wolf by the ears.

TERENCE *Phormio* III.ii.21. The character in the comedy, Antipho, can't let go, yet can't hold on either.

aurī sacra famēs
~ accursed greed for gold.

VIRGIL *Aeneid* iii.57. Aeneas tells how Priam, fearing that his city of Troy might fall, sent Polydorus, his youngest son, with a vast weight of gold, to the protection of the king of Thrace. The latter, in violation of the sacred rules of hospitality, killed him in order to get the money.

aut amat aut ōdit mulier, nihil est tertium
~ a woman either loves or hates, there is no third course.

PUBLILIUS SYRUS *Sententiae* A.6.

aut Caesar aut nūllus (or nihil)
~ either Caesar (i.e. the emperor) or nobody (nothing), i.e. all or nothing.

Based on the words of Caligula quoted at SUETONIUS, *Caligula* xxxvii.1. The motto of Cesare Borgia.

aut īnsānit homō aut versūs facit
~ either the man is mad or he is writing poetry.

HORACE *Satires* II.vii.117. Cf. Dryden, *Absalom and Achitophel* I.163–4: 'Great wits are sure to madness near alli'd, And thin partitions do their bounds divide.'

aut inveniam viam aut faciam
~ either I shall find a way or I shall make one.

aut nōn tentāris aut perfice
~ either do not attempt or finish the job.

OVID *Ars Amatoria* i.389. The poet suggests that, if you feel you must seduce the maid of the woman you are really interested in, you must make a good job of it.

aut prōdesse volunt aut dēlectāre poētae
~ poets seek either to profit or to please.

HORACE *Ars Poetica* 333. This quotation suggests that to profit and to please are mutually exclusive alternatives, but in fact Horace's next line (334) makes it clear that a third option is to combine the two.

aut rēgem aut fatuum nāscī oportet
~ one should be born either king or fool.

A proverb quoted by SENECA (*Apocolocyntosis* i.1).

aut vincere aut morī
~ either to conquer or to die.

avē atque valē
~ hail and farewell; a greeting followed by a goodbye (*see* VALE).

CATULLUS ci.10. Writing to his brother who had died abroad at Troy, the poet concludes with the poignant words: *atque in perpetuum, frater, ave atque vale* (and for eternity, brother, hail and farewell).

avē, Caesar, moritūrī tē salūtant
~ hail, Caesar, men doomed to die salute thee.

The address of gladiators to the emperor at the start of the gladiatorial games.

avē Maria
~ Hail Mary! **a** the angel's salutation to the Virgin Mary, from St Luke's gospel i.28. **b** the first two words of a prayer to the Virgin as Mother of God, often set to music.

ā verbīs ad verbera
~ from words to blows.

avīto viret honōre
~ he is green with ancestral honours; such are the honours heaped on his forefathers that he **a** thrives on them **b** wears them like a laurel crown.

barba tenus sapientēs

~ literally, 'wise as far as the beard', i.e. with the appearance
of wisdom only.

beātae memoriae

~ of blessed memory.

Used on tombstones and memorials.

beātus ille quī procul negōtiīs ... paterna rūra bōbus exercet suīs

~ happy the man who far away from business ... tills with his
own oxen the fields his father owned.

HORACE *Epodes* ii.1–3. Horace's vision of an idyllic pastoral life far from
the madding crowd's ignoble strife proves deceptive. We discover in ll.
67–70 that these are the words of the moneylender Alfius who might
dally verbally with the rustic dream but in fact has no serious intention
of abandoning his ruthless business life in the city.

bella gerant aliī

~ let others wage war!

OVID *Heroides* xvii.254. Laodamia is writing to her husband Protesilaus
who is at the Trojan War. She begs him to stay out of danger, but he was
in fact the first Greek to die at Troy.

bella! horrida bella!

~ wars! terrible wars!

VIRGIL *Aeneid* vi.86. In a terrifying prophecy, Apollo's priestess, the Sibyl
at Cumae, foresees the grim warfare that Aeneas must wage in Italy; in l.
87, she says that she can see the river Tiber foaming with streams of
blood.

bellum nec timendum nec prōvocandum
∿ war must be neither feared nor provoked.

based on the praise of the emperor Trajan by PLINY (*Panegyricus* xvi.2) *non times bella nec provocas* (you do not fear wars and you do not provoke them).

bēlua multōrum capitum
∿ literally, 'monster with many heads', i.e. the mob with their manifold ignoble or shameful ambitions.

HORACE *Epistles* I.i.76.

beneficium accipere lībertātem est vendere
∿ to accept a favour is to sell one's liberty.

PUBLILIUS SYRUS *Sententiae* B.5.

bene quī latuit bene vīxit
∿ he who has successfully lived an obscure life has lived well.

OVID *Tristia* III.iv.25.

benignō nūmine
∿ with the gods (proving) favourable.

bibere venēnum in aurō
∿ to drink poison from a cup of gold.

bis dat qui cito dat
∿ he gives twice who gives swiftly; you double your payment by paying up speedily.

This proverb, quoted in a slightly different form by PUBLILIUS SYRUS (*Sententiae* 1.6), is echoed in English by Sir Francis Bacon and quoted by Cervantes in *Don Quixote*.

bis peccāre in bellō nōn licet
∿ one cannot blunder twice in war.

bis puerī senēs
∿ old men are children twice over; old age is a second childhood.

27

Cf. SHAKESPEARE, *As You Like It* II.vii.163–6:

> Last scene of all,
> That ends this strange eventful history,
> Is second childishness, and mere oblivion;
> Sans teeth, sans eyes, sans taste, sans every thing.

bis vīvit quī bene vīvit
∼ the man who lives well lives twice over.

blandae mendācia linguae
∼ the lies of a smooth tongue.

bonā fidē (adjective)
∼ (acting or done) in good faith, i.e. sincere, genuine.

First recorded use in English 1788.

1882 *Medical temperance Journal* L.83 The bona fide poor are benefited.

bona fidēs
∼ good faith, freedom from intent to deceive.

bonīs avibus
∼ literally, 'under good birds', i.e. under good auspices.

The flight of birds was often used as a sign of the gods' favour or the opposite.

bonus homō semper tīrō
∼ a good man is always a novice.

Based on MARTIAL XII.li.2.

bōs in linguā
∼ literally, 'an ox on the tongue', i.e. he she has been bribed or terrified into silence.

The proverbial expression occurs in Greek in AESCHYLUS *Agamemnon* 36–7, where the watchman, unable to speak out for fear, says that 'a great ox stands on his tongue'.

brevis esse labōrō, obscūrus fīō
∼ I labour to be brief, and I become obscure.

HORACE *Ars Poetica* 25–6. The brevity of the plain style may make it hard to understand.

brūtum fulmen

~ literally, 'an insensible thunderbolt', i.e. a mere noise, an ineffective act or empty threat.

PLINY *Natural History* II.xliii.

1603 C. HEYDON *A defence of judiciall astrologie*. 55 The counsels and decrees of the Church . . . prove *bruta fulmina*, making vain cracks without any touch of that which I defend.

c. or ca.

See CIRCA.

cadit quaestiō
> ~ the question drops, i.e. there can be no further discussion.

caeca invidia est
> ~ envy is blind.

LIVY (XXXVIII.xlix.5) is giving the speech of Manlius to the Senate in 187 BC in which he says that the blind jealousy which has denied him the celebration of a triumph for his military attainments knows nothing except how to belittle courageous deeds and to degrade honour and its rewards.

caelebs quid agam
> ~ (you wonder) what I, a bachelor, am up to.

HORACE *Odes* III.viii.1. The poet thinks that his patron Maecenas may be surprised that the preparations for a festival are being so busily conducted in a bachelor household. The reason is that he is paying a vow made to Bacchus when he escaped death from a falling tree.

caelum nōn animum mūtant quī trāns mare currunt
> ~ those who hurry across the sea change their sky (i.e. climate), not their attitude.

HORACE *Epistles* I.xi.27. The poem claims that the benefits of tourism are illusory. What matters is one's philosophy of living.

Caesar nōn suprā grammaticōs
> ~ Caesar has no authority over the grammarians.

A severe response to the words of Kaiser Sigismund who, on being told of an error of gender in his Latin, asserted, '*Ego sum Imperator Romanorum, et supra grammaticam*' (I am the Emperor of the Romans, and above grammar).

callida iūnctūra
~ a skilful setting, a clever collocation.

HORACE *Ars Poetica* 46–7. The poet says that the most effective way of stringing words together occurs when a familiar word is made new. An example from Horace is CARPE DIEM, when the common word *carpe* (seize, pluck) is used metaphorically to mean 'eagerly seize (what the day has to offer)'.

Campus Martius
~ the Field of Mars.

A vast park in Rome situated to the east of a bend in the Tiber, where activities included elections, sport, and military drill.

candida Pāx
~ white-robed Peace.

TIBULLUS I.x.45. The poet celebrates Peace as the creator of the fulfilled agricultural life.

cantābit vacuus cōram latrōne viātor
~ the empty-handed traveller will sing in the presence of the robber.

JUVENAL x.22. The poor man can take comfort in the fact that he has nothing to be stolen.

capāx imperiī nisi imperāsset
~ literally, 'capable of ruling had he not ruled', i.e. had he (Galba) never become emperor (he would have been judged) capable of the office.

TACITUS *Histories* i.49. This is Tacitus' devastating verdict on Galba who was one of the four Roman emperors (three of them, including Galba, extremely short-lived in that role) in AD 69.

See also CONSENSU OMNIUM.

captātiō benevolentiae
~ a bid for the goodwill of hearers or readers.

carpe diem, quam minimum crēdula posterō (often simply: carpe diem)
~ seize the day, trusting as little as possible to the morrow.

HORACE *Odes* I.xi.8. In these celebrated words, the poet urges Leuconoë to make the most of the present and steer clear of astrologers.

1817 BYRON *Letter* 2 Jan. in Moore *Life* (1830) II.68 I never anticipate—*carpe diem*—the past at least is one's own, which is one reason for making sure of the present.

casta est quam nēmō rogāvit
~ she is chaste whom nobody has propositioned.

OVID *Amores* I.viii.43

casus bellī
~ an act justifying, or regarded as a reason for, war.

1849 J. S. MILL in *Westminster Review* LI.28 To assist a people struggling for liberty . . . is not a *casus belli* set down in Vattel.

causa sine quā nōn
~ an indispensable condition.

cavē
~ (school slang) beware!

A signal of warning, e.g. of the approach of a teacher. Pronounced like the letters KV.

1584 R. GREENE *Carde of Fancie* 7 Now thou wilt cry Cave when thy coin is consumed and beware when thy wealth is wracked.

Also in **keep cavē**, keep watch for approach of teacher. First recorded use in English 1868.

1906 E. NESBIT *Railway Children* xiv.295 He won't keep *cave*, shirks his turn And says he came to school to learn!

caveat
~ let him/her beware.

Also in **to enter a caveat**, to give a warning.

1577 tr. *Bullinger's Decades* (1592) 405 It pleased the goodness of God by giving the law to put in a caveat . . . for the tranquility of mankind.

caveat ēmptor
~ 'let the buyer beware', let him keep his eyes open (for once entered upon, the bargain is binding).

1523 J. FITZHERBERT *Husbandry* f. xxxvi He [sc. the horse] is no chapman's ware if he be wild: but and he be tame and have been ridden upon then caveat emptor beware thou buyer.

cavē canem
~ beware of the dog.

cavendō tūtus
~ safe by being on one's guard.

cavē nē lit(t)erās Bellerophontis adferās

∿ take care that the letter you carry is not your death warrant (literally, 'a letter of Bellerophon').

Falsely accused of making sexual overtures to Proitos' wife, Bellerophon was sent by Proitos to the King of Lycia, the wife's father, carrying a letter which, unbeknown to its bearer, urged the recipient to put him to death (HOMER *Iliad* vi.169–70, 178). This is the first reference to writing in Western literature. In Shakespeare's play, Hamlet is sent by his uncle Claudius to the King of England with such a letter (*Hamlet* IV.iii.66–8).

cēdant arma togae

∿ let arms yield to the toga, i.e. let military power yield to civil power.

CICERO *De Officiis* I.xxii.77. Insisting on the superiority of political mastery to military force, Cicero praises his own achievement in quelling Catiline's rebellion (63 BC): 'What achievement in war was ever so great? What triumph can be compared with it?'

cēdō maiōrī

∿ I yield to a greater person.

Based on MARTIAL *De Spectaculis* 32. It is better to be second to a greater person than to an inferior one.

certum est quia impossible est

∿ it is certain because it is impossible.

See CREDO QUIA ABSURDUM/IMPOSSIBILE EST.

cētera dēsunt

∿ the remainder is missing.

cēterīs (or caeterīs) paribus

∿ other things being equal.

1601 T. WRIGHT *Passions* Preface A 4 b Yet my meaning is alwayes *caeteris paribus*, because [etc.].

cf.

See CONFER.

circā (c. or ca.)

∿ about.

Often used with dates.

1861 *National Review* Oct. 307 A curious photograph of a rustic family at work, *circa* 1390.

cīvis Rōmānus sum
~ I am a Roman citizen.

CICERO *In Verrem* II.v.162. The plea of being a Roman citizen was supposed to be enough to stop beatings, since by the Valerian law such a citizen could not be bound and by the Sempronian law it was forbidden to scourge him or to beat him with rods. Cicero draws attention to the monstrousness of Verres, the brutal governor of Sicily, by dwelling on a flagrant transgression of these laws.

St Paul, when a centurion commanded him 'to be examined by scourging', in effect made the plea of '*Civis Romanus sum*' when he asked, 'Is it lawful for you to scourge a Roman citizen, and uncondemned?' He was sent to Rome to be judged by the emperor Nero (Acts of the Apostles xxii.25–9).

clārior ē tenebrīs
~ the brighter from the darkness, i.e. the surrounding darkness emphasizes the light.

clārum et venerābile nōmen
~ a glorious and venerable name.

LUCAN *De Bello Civili* ix.202. Lucan puts these words into the mouth of Cato the Younger as he pays a tribute to the dead Pompey, the hero of the poem.

cōgitō, ergō sum
~ I think, therefore I am.

The first principle in philosophy posited by Descartes.

coitus interruptus
~ sexual intercourse in which, with the intention of avoiding conception, the penis is completely withdrawn from the vagina before ejaculation.

1900 H. HAVELOCK ELLIS *Studies in the Psychology of Sex* II.127 Onan's device was not auto-erotic, but was an early example of withdrawal before emission or *coitus interruptus*.

coitus reservātus
~ sexual intercourse in which, by a technique of deliberate control, ejaculation or complete orgasm is avoided and copulation thereby prolonged.

1903 H. HAVELOCK ELLIS *Studies in the Psychology of Sex* III.248 We practiced all sorts of fancy coitus, *coitus reservatus*, etc.

commūne bonum

∼ the common good.

compos mentis

∼ having control of one's mind, in one's right mind.

1679 *Trials of Wakeman, etc.* 55 I was scarce *Compos mentis*.

concordia discors

∼ discordant harmony.

HORACE *Epistles* I.xii.19. The poet visualizes a friend of his reflecting on physics (nature's discordant harmony).

conditiō sine quā nōn

∼ literally, 'a condition without which (it can) not (be)', i.e. an indispensable condition.

See SINE QUA NON.

cōnfer (abbreviated to cf.)

∼ compare.

coniūnctīs vīribus

∼ with united powers.

cōnscia mēns rēctī

∼ a mind conscious of its innocence.

OVID *Fasti* iv.311. Unjustified rumours circulate about a beautiful Roman noblewoman called Claudia Quinta because she dresses pleasingly and varies her hairstyle. Conscious of her chastity, she laughs at the lying talk.

cōnsēnsus facit lēgem

∼ consent makes the law.

cōnsēnsū omnium

∼ by the agreement of all.

A famous usage of this phrase is Tacitus' description of Galba (*c.* 3 BC–AD 69), for a brief while emperor (*Histories* i.49): *omnium cōnsēnsū capāx imperiī nisi imperāsset* (by the agreement of all capable of being emperor, had he not actually become emperor). Everyone thought he had the qualities for the position, but when he attained it he proved inadequate.

cōnsule Plancō

~ when Plancus was consul, i.e. when I was a young man.

HORACE *Odes* III.xiv.28. Lucius Munatius Plancus had been consul in 42 BC, the year of the battle of Philippi in which the twenty-two-year-old Horace had fought on the losing side. The times—and the poet—have quietened down between then and the publication of this poem, probably about 23 BC.

cōnsummātum est

~ it is completed.

Christ's last words on the cross (John xix.30).

cōnstrūctiō ad sēnsum

~ a construction on the basis of the sense, i.e. one in which the requirements of a grammatical form are overridden by those of a word-meaning.

E.g. the construction of a collective noun in the singular with the plural form of a verb because the noun denotes a plurality. An example: 'a number of people say that . . .' when the singular word 'number' may seem to demand 'says'.

1894 B. L. GILDERSLEEVE *Latin Grammar* (edn 3) 148 The natural relation is preferred to the artificial (*constructio ad sensum, per synesin*, according to the sense).

contrā mundum

~ against the world, defying or opposing everyone.

1766 LORD CHESTERFIELD LETTER 9 Dec. (1932) VI.2787 Even *he* cannot be alone, *contra mundum*.

contrāria contrāriīs cūrantur

~ opposites are cured by opposites.

cōpia verbōrum

~ fluency of speech.

cōram populō

~ before the public.

Corpus Christī

~ literally, 'the body of Christ'.

Used of the Feast of the Blessed Sacrament or Body of Christ, observed on the Thursday after Trinity Sunday. In many places (e.g. at York and

Coventry) it was regularly celebrated by performance of the sacred plays or pageants: hence *Corpus Christi play*. There are colleges at both Cambridge and Oxford called Corpus Christi.

1377 LANGLAND *Piers Plowman* B. xv.381 As clerkes in corpus-christ feste singen & reden.

corpus dēlictī
∼ literally, 'the body of the crime', i.e. the concrete evidence of a crime, especially the body of a murdered person.

1863 *N. Y. State Court of Appeals, Rep.* IV.179 The *corpus delicti*, in murder, has two components, death as the result and the criminal agency of another as the means.

corpus vīle
∼ literally, 'cheap body'.

Used of a living or dead body that is of so little value that it can be used for experiment without regard for the outcome; also experimental material of any kind, or something which has no value except as the object of experimentation.

1822 T. DE QUINCEY *Confessions of an opium-eater* App. 189 *Fiat experimentum in corpore vili* [let the experiment be done on a cheap (or worthless) body] is a just rule where there is any reasonable presumption of benefit to arise on a large scale.

1953 *Essays in Criticism* III.i.4 I am not proposing to include among these initial *corpora vilia* [plural of *corpus vile*] passages from either Mr Eliot's criticism or Dr Leavis's.

corrigenda
∼ things to be corrected, especially errors or faults in printing, of which corrections are given.

1850 A. JUDSON in Wayland *A memoir of the life and labors of the Rev. A. Judson* (1853) II.v.170 I received thankfully yours of 28th January accompanied by a list of corrigenda.

corruptiō optimī pessima
∼ the corruption of the best is the worst (of all corruptions).

cor ūnum, via ūna
∼ one heart, one way.

crambē repetīta
∼ cold cabbage warmed up.

JUVENAL (vii.154), echoing a Greek proverb δὶς κράμβη θάνατος (cabbage (boiled) twice is death), talks about the repetitiousness of the exercises at the rhetorical schools which kills off the wretched masters. Sir Walter Scott (*The Monastery*, Introduction) uses a variant, *crambē bis cocta* (cabbage boiled twice): 'There was a disadvantage in treading this Border district, for it had been already ransacked by the author himself, as well as by others; and, unless presented under a new light, was likely to afford ground to the objection of *Crambe bis cocta*.'

crēdat Iūdaeus Apella, nōn ego
~ let the Jew Apella believe that, for I don't, i.e. tell that to the marines.

HORACE *Satires* I.v.100. On his famous journey to Brundisium the poet found it ridiculous when the people of Gnatia (Egnatia) tried to persuade him that the frankincense at the temple's threshold melted without fire. The Romans regarded the Jews as particularly superstitious.

crēdō quia absurdum/impossibile est
~ I believe it because it is absurd/impossible.

Based on TERTULLIAN *De Carne Christi* 5.

crēdula rēs amor est
~ a credulous thing is love.

crēscite et multiplicāminī
~ increase and multiply.

The motto of the State of Maryland.

crēscit eundō
~ it grows as it goes.

LUCRETIUS *De Rerum Naturae* vi.341. The poet, talking about a thunderbolt, explains that its velocity increases as it moves. The motto of New Mexico.

crīmen falsī
~ the crime of perjury.

crocum in Ciliciam ferre
~ to carry saffron to Cilicia, i.e. to carry coals to Newcastle, to do something which is completely superfluous.

Cilicia had plenty of saffron, and Newcastle plenty of coal.

crux (criticōrum)
~ puzzle (of critics), a difficulty which it torments or troubles one greatly to interpret or explain, a thing that puzzles the ingenuity, e.g. a textual crux.

1718 T. SHERIDAN *To Swift* in *Works* (1814) XV.56 Dear dean, since in cruxes and puns you and I deal, Pray, Why is a woman a sieve and a riddle? J. SWIFT *To Sheridan* ibid. 61 As for your new rebus, or riddle, or crux, I will either explain, or repay it in trucks.

cucullus nōn facit monāchum
~ literally, 'the cowl does not make the monk', i.e. do not judge men by what they appear to be.

A medieval Latin proverb, quoted by Shakespeare in *Measure for Measure* (V.i.261) and *Twelfth Night* (I.v.61–2).

cui bonō?
~ for whose advantage? who stood to gain?

CICERO (*Pro Milone* 32) mentions Lucius Cassius Longinus (tribune of the people in 137 BC) who, when presiding in court, always urged the jurors to vote with this in mind. Today the expression is more usually taken as meaning 'to what end?' 'of what use?'

cum
~ with, together with.

First recorded use in English 1589.

1871–3 A. TROLLOPE *Eustace Diamonds* (1873) I.xiii.173 The Belgravia-cum-Pimlico life.

cum grānō salis (or simply cum grānō)
~ with a grain of salt, with some caution or reserve.

1653 BAXTER *Chr. Concord* 64 I know this speech must be understood *cum grano salis*.

cum laude
See MAGNA CUM LAUDE.

cum tacent, clāmant
~ while they are silent, they shout.

CICERO *In Catilinam* I.xxi. Cicero interprets the silence of the Senate as a shrieking denunciation of Catiline.

cūnctandō restituit rem
~ he restored the state by delaying.

ENNIUS *Annals* xii.363. Ennius pays tribute to the great Quintus Fabius Maximus Cunctator (= delayer), who saved Rome by refusing to engage in pitched battle with Hannibal, her greatest enemy. Cicero, Seneca, and Virgil all quote these famous words.

39

cūria pauperibus clausa est

~ the senate house is closed to the poor.

OVID *Amores* III.viii.55. The poet stresses the effectiveness of money.

cūriōsa fēlīcitās

~ literally, 'careful felicity', i.e. a studied felicity of expression.

Applied by Eumolpus, a poet in the *Satyricon* by Petronius Arbiter (118), to Horace's style.

1752 LORD CHESTERFIELD *Letter* 16 Mar. (1774) II.229 The delicacy and *curiosa felicitas* of that poet [sc. Horace].

currente calamō

~ literally, 'with the pen running on', i.e. offhand, extempore, without premeditation.

The actual phrase is not recorded in classical Latin.

1776 W. MASON *Letter* 25 Mar. in *Walpole's Correspondence* (1955) XXVIII.254 What I here send you was written yesterday *currente calamo*.

curriculum vītae

~ a brief account of one's career.

1902 *New International Encyclopedia* III.21/2 Anciently biography was more of a mere *curriculum vitae* than it is now.

custōs mōrum

~ guardian of manners (or of morals).

dabit deus hīs quoque fīnem
~ to these things too god will grant an end.

VIRGIL *Aeneid* i.199. Putting a brave face on things, Aeneas tells his followers not to be too downcast by the storm that has driven them off course to the coast of Africa. They have survived worse in the past.

dā dextram miserō
~ give the right hand to the unhappy.

dā locum meliōribus
~ give place to your betters.

TERENCE *Phormio* III.ii.37.

damnant quod nōn intellegunt
~ they condemn what they do not understand.

data et accepta
~ expenditure and receipts.

date obolum Belisāriō
~ give an obol (a penny—an obol was a small Greek coin) to Belisarius.

Belisarius was the greatest of the emperor Justinian's generals. Accused in AD 563 of conspiring against Justinian's life, he was stripped of all his property and his eyes were put out. Thus reduced to beggary, as the story goes, he fastened a bag to his roadside hut and inscribed these words above it.

Dāvus sum, nōn Oedipus
~ I am Davus, not Oedipus i.e. I'm just an ordinary man, and no good at riddles.

TERENCE *Andria* I.ii.23. Oedipus solved the riddle of the Sphinx and thus brought an end to her terrorizing of the Thebans. What, asked the Sphinx, has four legs in the morning, two at noon, and three in the evening? Oedipus gave the correct answer: man (who crawls on all fours in his infancy, stands upright on two legs in his maturity, and walks with a stick in his old age).

dē asinī umbrā disceptāre
~ to fight over an ass's shadow, i.e. to fight over trifles.

Demosthenes tells the tale of how a fight developed when, under a hot sun, the owner of an ass disputed with the man to whom he had hired it over who had the right to sit in its shadow.

deciēns repetīta placēbit
~ it will give pleasure when looked at afresh for the tenth time.

HORACE *Ars Poetica* 365. The poet is here talking about paintings—some are only worth a single look while others repay many viewings—and he says that poems are like that too.

dēcrēvī
~ I have decreed.

decus et tūtāmen
~ an adornment and a means of protection.

A quotation from Virgil's *Aeneid* (v.262), where it refers to a fine corselet or cuirass, this was the motto on the rim of the English crown coin. It is still used on the English pound coin.

1688 T. SHADWELL *The squire of Alsatia* ii.*Works* (1720) IV.48 To equip you with some Meggs, Smelts, Decus's and Georges.

dē diē in diem
~ from day to day.

dē duōbus malīs, minus est semper ēligendum
~ of two evils, the lesser is always to be chosen.

Thomas à Kempis' version of a sentence in Aristotle in which this is recommended as a second-best course (*Nicomachean Ethics* II.ix.1109a). Cf. CICERO *De Officiis* III.xxix *minima de malis* (of evils (choose) the least).

dē factō
~ in reality.

First recorded use in English 1602.

1638 W. CHILLINGWORTH. *Religion of Protestants* I.iii. para. 30 He may doe it *de facto*, but *de iure* he cannot. *See* DE IURE.

dēgenerēs animōs timor arguit
∼ cowardice proves that a man's spirit is base.

VIRGIL *Aeneid* iv.13. Dido has listened to Aeneas' story of his deeds during the fall of Troy and his subsequent adventures. She concludes from his intrepid spirit that he must be a supremely noble hero.

dē gustibus nōn est disputandum
∼ there is no disputing about tastes, every man to his taste.

Cf. French *chacun à son goût* (each to his taste) and English 'there's no accounting for tastes'.

Deī grātiā
∼ by the grace of God.

Introduced into English charters in 1106, to signify 'by the grace of god as opposed to man's appointment'. On British coins, the monarch is declared '*D.G. (Dei gratia) REX* (or *REG(ina)*)' (King (or Queen) by the grace of God).

dē integrō
∼ anew, over again from the start.

dē iūre
∼ sanctioned by law.

Nearly always opposed to DE FACTO.

dēlenda est Carthāgō
∼ Carthage must be destroyed.

The words with which Cato the Elder concluded all his speeches in the Roman senate. Carthage was Rome's most dangerous enemy. Eventually Cato's wish was fulfilled when that city was destroyed in 146 BC, but he had died in 149. His words are proverbial and signify that something that stands in the way of our greatness must be eliminated whatever the cost.

dēlīrium tremēns
∼ a species of delirium induced by excessive indulgence in alcohol, and characterized by tremblings and various delusions of the senses.

1813 T. SUTTON (title) Tracts on Delirium Tremens, etc., etc.

dē minimīs nōn cūrat lēx

~ the law does not concern itself about very small matters.

F. BACON *Letter* 282.

dē mortuīs nīl nisi bonum

~ of the dead (say) nothing but good, i.e. speak no ill of the dead.

The Latin derives from a Greek saying attributed to the Spartan ephor or civil magistrate Chilon (sixth century BC).

dē nihilō nihilum, in nihilum nīl posse revertī

~ nothing can come from nothing, nothing can return to nothing.

PERSIUS iii.84. The poet represents an uncouth soldier pouring Philistine scorn on this, the fundamental principle of the Epicurean philosophy.

Deō adiuvante

~ God assisting, with God's help.

Deō favente

~ God favouring, with God's favour.

Deō grātiās

~ thanks (be) to God.

dē omnī rē scībilī et quibusdam aliīs

~ concerning everything that can be known and some other things too.

To the riskily comprehensive title of the fifteenth-century Italian scholar Pico della Mirandola's work *De Omni Re Scibili* (concerning everything that can be known), some satirical spirit, possible Voltaire, added *et quibusdam aliis* in order to mock della Mirandola's pretensions.

Deō volente (abbreviated to DV)

~ God willing, if nothing prevents (the fulfilment of a promise).

1767 T. GRAY *Letter* 6 June in *Works* (1884) III.268 My intention is (*Deo volente*) to come to Cambridge on Friday or Saturday next.

dēprendī miserum est

~ it's tough to be caught.

HORACE *Satires* I.ii.134.

dē profundīs

~ up from the depths (I have cried to thee, Lord).

The opening words of Psalm 129 in the Vulgate. They are sung by Roman Catholics when the dead are committed to the grave. Oscar Wilde used them as the title for his great lament (1897) about the circumstances which had led to his imprisonment.

dēsine fāta deum flectī spērāre precandō

~ stop hoping that what is fated by the gods can be altered by prayers.

VIRGIL *Aeneid* vi.376. Despite his plea, the unburied helmsman Palinurus cannot yet find rest in the underworld since he has not been buried. The Cumaean Sibyl is unable to alter what fate decrees, but reassures him that he will be buried soon.

dēsipere in locō

~ to let go (have a wild time) on occasion.

HORACE *Odes* IV.xii.28. Spring is here. Horace invites his fellow poet Virgil to visit him and drink a cask of wine with him. It is pleasant to let oneself go now and again, he says.

dēsunt cetera

~ the remainder is missing.

dē tē fābula nārrātur

~ the story is about you.

HORACE *Satires* I.i.69–70. Horace asks his reader why he smiles at the myth of Tantalus who can never drink the water which constantly evades his lips; *mutato nomine* (i.e. by changing your name for that of Tantalus) the story is about you (the reader) in your obsession with money.

deus absconditus

~ a god who is hidden (from man).

1932 *Character & Personality* Sept. 51 Where ... in the annals of Victorianism is the sentimental god of the nineteenth century ever faced with a *deus absconditus* as in Luther's teaching?

deus ex māchinā

~ (a) god (let down) from the theatre crane, i.e. the device by which gods were suspended above the stage in the Greek theatre.

The expression can also refer to a power, event, person, or thing that comes in the nick of time to solve a difficulty, especially in a novel or play.

Brewer writes scathingly: 'any forced incident, such as the arrival of a rich uncle from the Indies to help a young couple in their pecuniary embarrassments.'

1697 J. SERGEANT *Solid Philos.* 136 Nor is it at all allowable to Philosophy to bring in a *Deus e Machina* at every turn when our selves are at a loss to give a Reason for our *Thesis*. [*e* is a variant spelling of *ex*]

deus nōbīs haec ōtia fēcit
∼ it is a god that hath given us this relaxation.

VIRGIL *Eclogues* I.6. Octavian, later to become the emperor Augustus, has allowed Virgil's pastoral character Tityrus to keep his farm—and thus to have the leisure to play his pipe under a spreading beech-tree—at a time when vast areas of land are being confiscated to settle the troops who had fought for Octavian and Mark Antony at the battle of Philippi (42 BC). Tityrus here pays extravagant tribute to his benefactor.

This is the somewhat improbable motto of Liverpool.

Deus vōbīscum!
∼ God be with you!

Deus vult
∼ God wills it.

The cry of the people at the beginning of the First Crusade when they were addressed by Pope Urban II at the Council of Clermont in 1095. The crusaders were successful in taking the Holy Land from the Muslims.

dictum sapientī sat est
∼ a word to the wise is enough.

Usually quoted as *verbum* rather than *dictum*.

PLAUTUS *Persa* IV.vii.19.

diem perdidī
∼ I have lost a day.

SUETONIUS *Titus* viii.1. Illustrating the kindness of the emperor Titus, Suetonius relates how he uttered these words when on one occasion at dinner he remembered that he had done nothing for anybody all that day.

Diēs Irae
∼ Day of Wrath.

The first words of a well-known medieval hymn about the Last Judgement. The probable author was the Franciscan Thomas of Celano, born in Abruzzi in Italy, who died in 1255.

diēs nōn

~ a non-business day.

A legal phrase referring to a day when the courts do not sit.

difficile est satiram nōn scrībere

~ it is difficult not to write satire.

JUVENAL i.30.

digitō mōnstrārī et dīcier 'hic est'

~ to be pointed at and to have people say, 'It's him.'

PERSIUS i.28. The poet evokes the pleasure of notoriety.

dī nōs quasi pilās hominēs habent

~ the gods hold us humans like balls in their hands.

PLAUTUS *Captivi* 22. We are the playthings of the gods. Cf. John Webster, *The Duchess of Malfi* V.iv.54–5: 'We are merely the stars' tennis-balls, struck and banded Which way please them.'

dīra Necessitās

~ grim Necessity.

HORACE *Odes* III.xxiv.6. However wealthy you may be, this is one thing that you cannot escape.

dīs aliter vīsum est

~ literally, 'it seemed otherwise to the gods', i.e. the gods thought otherwise.

VIRGIL *Aeneid* ii.428. In his account of the sack of Troy, Aeneas tells of the death of Rhipeus, the most just and righteous of all the Trojans. Clearly, Aeneas reflects in this bitter parenthesis, the gods did not share this estimate of him. John Dryden (1631–1700) translates: 'Heav'n thought not so.'

disiecta membra

~ scattered limbs.

An inaccurately quoted reference to the end of the third book of Ovid's *Metamorphoses* (*membra . . . derepta*, I. 731) where the fate of Pentheus, who was torn to pieces by the female worshippers of Bacchus, including his mother, is decribed. Its use to refer to 'bleeding chunks' of excerpted poetry is based on Horace (*Satires* I.iv.62): *disiecti membra poetae* (the limbs of the dismembered poet). Referring to the early Roman poet Ennius (239–169 BC), he says that you can tell from the briefest of extracts from his work that you are dealing with a true poet.

dīvide et imperā
~ divide and rule.

The motto of Louis XI of France. Though this political axiom—conveying that government is more easily maintained if factions are set against each other and not permitted to unite against the ruler—is attributed to the Florentine political philosopher Niccolo Machiavelli (1469–1527), he in fact denounced it.

dīxī
~ I have spoken, i.e. that is the end of my speech—and the end of the matter.

dīxit
~ an utterance (quoted as) already given.

1628 JOHN EARLE *Micro-cosmographie* 66 He hates authority as the tyrant of reason, and you cannot anger him worse than with a father's dixit.

docendō discimus
~ by teaching we learn.

This is a crisper formulation of SENECA *Letters* vii.8: *homines dum docent discunt* (while they teach, men learn).

dolī capāx
~ literally, 'capable of an unlawful act', i.e. capable of having the evil intention necessary for the commission of a crime.

1676 SIR MATTHEW HALE *Historia Placitorum Coronae* I. 22 He might or might not be guilty according to the circumstances of the fact that might induce the court and jury to judge him *doli capax, vel incapax* [capable of an unlawful act, or incapable].

Domine, dīrige nōs
~ Lord, direct us.

The motto of the City of London.

Dominus illūminātiō mea
~ the Lord is my light.

The motto of Oxford University.

Dominus vōbīscum!
~ the Lord be with you!

domus et placēns uxor
~ a home and a pleasing wife.

HORACE *Odes* II.xiv.21–2. In a famous poem about the passing of time, Horace tells Postumus that he will have to leave his home and his family when he dies.

dōnec eris sospes, multōs numerābis amīcōs
~ while all is well with you, you will possess (literally, 'count') many friends.

OVID *Tristia* I.ix.5. The point is that when trouble strikes, such fair-weather friends will desert you.

drāmatis persōnae
~ the characters in a drama or play.

1730 H. FIELDING *Temple Beau* 1.vi in *Works* (1882) VIII.117 There is (to give you a short Dramatis Personae) my worthy uncle [etc.].

dūcit amor patriae
~ love of country leads (me).

ductus litterārum
~ the general shape and formation of letters and their combinations in the manuscripts, study of which may make possible the restoration of true readings in a corrupt text.

1888 *Athenaeum* 7 Jan. 25/1 Of all our literature there is none more carelessly printed than our early drama—none in which conjecture, founded on the *ductus litterarum*, comes more legitimately into play for the correction of its errors.

dūcunt volentem fāta
~ the Fates lead the willing man.

SENECA *Letters* cvii.11. While they lead the willing man, they drag the unwilling (*nolentem trahunt*).

dulce 'domum'
~ a sweet thing, home.

From a song sung at English schools just before the holidays. It was reportedly composed by a boy of St Mary's College, Winchester.

dulce est dēsipere in locō
~ it is delightful to let go (i.e. have a wild time) on occasion.

See DESIPERE IN LOCO.

dulce et decōrum est prō patriā morī
~ it is sweet and honourable to die for one's fatherland.

HORACE *Odes* III.ii.13. These words, now thought to be intended ironically by Horace, are memorably quoted by Wilfred Owen in '*Dulce et Decorum Est*', his poem about a gas attack in the First World War. If you could have seen and heard the victim of the attack, he writes,

My friend, you would not tell with such high zest
To children ardent for some desperate glory,
The old Lie: Dulce et decorum est
Pro patria mori.

dum fāta sinunt, vīvite laetī

~ while the fates allow it, live happily.

SENECA *Hercules Furens* 178.

dum loquor, hōra fugit

~ while I am talking, time is flying.

OVID *Amores* I.xi.15. Ovid does not want to delay in advancing the progress of a love affair.

dum Rōma dēlīberat, Saguntum perit

~ while Rome deliberates, Saguntum is dying.

Based on LIVY XXI.vii.1. Despite futile deliberations about what they could do to help, the Romans left the Spanish city of Saguntum to be captured by the Carthaginian Hannibal.

dum spīrō, spērō

~ while I breathe, I hope, i.e. while there's life, there's hope.

Part of the motto of South Carolina.

dum tacent, clāmant

~ while they are silent, they shout, i.e. their silence is highly significant. *See* CUM TACENT, CLAMANT.

dum vīvimus, vīvāmus

~ while we live, let us live (to the full).

The Epicurean motto of the non-conformist divine, Philip Doddridge. Doddridge (1702–51) converted his motto into the following epigram, which was highly praised by Samuel Johnson:

'Live, while you live,' the epicure would say,
'And seize the pleasures of the present day.'
'Live, while you live,' the sacred preacher cries,
'And give to God each moment as it flies.'
Lord, in *my* view let each united be;
I live in pleasure while I live to thee.

dux fēmina factī

~ it was a woman who took the lead in the action.

VIRGIL *Aeneid* i.364. In Virgil's poem, Venus tells Aeneas how Dido showed spirited qualities of dynamic action when she fled with a group of refugees from her brutal brother's kingdom.

E

ecce homō!
~ Behold the man!

John xix.5 in the Vulgate. Pontius Pilate, the Roman governor of Judaea, showed Christ, bound with ropes and wearing a crown of thorns, to the people with these words. It has proved a favourite subject with painters.

ecce iterum Crispīnus
~ look, it's Crispinus again.

JUVENAL iv.1. Juvenal says he is returning to his attack on the appalling Crispinus. The phrase is used to mean 'I am returning to a topic which I have dealt with often before'.

ecce signum!
~ Behold the proof!

SHAKESPEARE 1 *Henry IV* II.iv.164–7 [Falstaff says] 'I am eight times thrust through the doublet, four through the hose; my buckler cut through and through, my saw hacked like a handsaw—*ecce signum!*'

ē (or ā) contrāriō
~ from a contrary position (especially in argument); in opposition; by dint of opposition or antagonism.

First recorded use in English 1602.

1957 H. F. JOLOWICZ *Roman Foundatins of Modern Law* ii.18 It is also subject to the argument *e contrario*. Words expressly applying a rule to one case may be held impliedly to exclude it in others.

ēditiō prīnceps
~ the first printed edition of a book.

1802 T. F. DIBDIN *An introduction to the knowledge of rare and valuable editions of the Greek and Latin* 4 This editio princeps contains but nine comedies.

e.g.

See EXEMPLI GRATIA.

ego et rēx meus

∼ I and my king.

The declaration of Cardinal Wolsey (?1475–1530). Wolsey came to regret his loyalty to his king. His last words were: 'Had I but served God as diligently as I have served the King, he would not have given me over in my gray hairs' (George Cavendish, *Negotiations of Thomas Wolsey* (1641), p. 113). Wolsey had innocently but unwisely used the formula *ego et rex meus* at various times. It was exploited in the accusation against him by the House of Lords, being viewed as an assertion that he was 'more like a fellow' to the king than a subject. Shakespeare in *Henry VIII* (III.ii.313–6) follows the exaggerated accusation given in Hall's *Chronicle*:

... in all you writ to Rome, or else
To foreign princes, 'Ego et Rex meus'
Was still inscrib'd; in which you brought the King
To be your servant.

Shakespeare gives the famous last words as:

Had I but serv'd my God with half the zeal
I serv'd my King, he would not in mine age
Have left me naked to mine enemies.   (III.ii.455–7)

ēheu! fugācēs lābuntur annī

∼ alas! the fleeting years slip by.

HORACE *Odes* II.xiv.1–2. In this famous ode, addressed to Postumus, Horace stresses the fugitive brevity of human life.

eiusdem farīnae

∼ of the same flour, i.e. (one) of the same sort (of person).

eiusdem generis

∼ of the same kind.

1663 S. BUTLER *Hudibras* I.i.65 A just comparison still is, Of things *ejusdem generis*.

1987 *Daily Telegraph* 10 Aug. 13/6 'Other records' ... had to be construed *eiusdem generis* with 'ledgers, day books, cash books and account books' and unsorted bundles of cheques and paying-in slips were not 'other records' within the meaning of the Act.

ējaculātiō praecōx

∼ premature ejaculation, rapid termination of the sexual act on the part of the male.

ēmeritus

~ honourably discharged from service.

Chiefly used in the phrase *emeritus professor*, the title given to a university professor who has retired from the office.

ēmūnctae nāris

~ literally, '(a man) of well-cleared nostril', i.e. a man of nice discernment.

eō ipsō

~ by that very act or quality, through that alone, thereby.

1696 J. SERGEANT *Method of Science* 1.v.50 Nothing can be said to be *Divisible*, or capable to be made *more*, but it must be said *eo ipso* to be Actually and truly *One*.

eō nōmine

~ under that name, i.e. explicitly.

1627 *Letter* 23 Nov. in Birch *Court & Times Charles. I* (1848) I.292 The Earl of Bridgewater hath, *eo nomine*, disbursed £10,000.

epistula nōn ērubēscit

~ a letter does not blush.

CICERO *Ad Familiares* V.xii.1. Cicero asks L. Lucceius to write an epic poem about his consulship. In the event, Cicero had to write this himself!

ē plūribus ūnum

~ one out of many.

Before 1956 regarded as the motto of the United States, a unity formed by many states.

ē rē nāta

~ under present circumstances.

ergō

~ therefore.

First recorded use in English 1400.

1846 W. GREENER *The science of gunnery* 343 'Ergo' says one, if a 56lb. ball can be thrown 3¼ miles, certain a 68lb. ball can be thrown further, for 'weight is power'.

ergō bibāmus

~ therefore let us drink.

errāre hūmānum est

~ to err is human.

Based on JEROME *Letters* lvii.12. Cf. 'Good-Nature and Good-Sense must ever join; To Err is Humane; to Forgive, Divine' (A. POPE *Essay on Criticism* i.525).

ēsse oportet ut vīvās, nōn vīvere ut edās

~ you ought to eat in order to live, not live in order to eat.

[CICERO] *Rhetorica ad Herennium* iv.39. This apophthegm is given as an example of chiasmus.

esse quam vidērī

~ to be rather than to seem.

est deus in nōbīs

~ there is a god inside us.

OVID *Ars Amatoria* iii.549 and *Fasti* vi.5.

est modus in rēbus

~ there is a limit in things, e.g. moderation should be observed, keep to the happy mean.

HORACE *Satires* I.i.106.

estō perpetua

~ may you last for ever.

Believed to be the final words of the philosopher and historian Fra Paolo Sarpi (1552–1623), they were addressed to his native Venice.

est quaedam flēre voluptās

~ there is a certain pleasure in weeping.

OVID *Tristia* IV.iii.37. Ovid writes from his exile on the Black Sea, encouraging his wife to lament for her loss of him. Tears bring their own relief.

et al. (abbreviation of et aliī (masculine), et aliae (feminine), and et alia (neuter)

~ and others.

Used especially to avoid giving a list of authors, etc., in full.

First recorded use in English 1883.

1962 G. K. HUNTER *John Lyly* ii.39 Lyly no doubt completed his school career ... having read, construed and explicated innumerable passages of Ovid, Cicero, Virgil, *et al.*

et cēterae/etcētera (usually abbreviated to etc.)
~ and the rest, and so forth, and so on.

et hoc (or id) genus omne
~ and all that sort of thing.

1748 LORD CHESTERFIELD *Letter* 9 Mar. (1774) I.271 All the shops, drolls, tumblers, rope-dancers, and *hoc genus omne*.

et in Arcadiā ego
~ I too dwell in Arcadia.

This inscription from the tomb in Nicolas Poussin's picture, *The Arcadian Shepherds*, makes the point that death is present even in the idyllic pastoral landscape of Arcadia in southern Greece. As a saying, however, these words are generally, though wrongly, taken to mean that 'I also had my time of bliss', 'I also lived in Arcadia'.

et scelerātīs sōl oritur
~ the sun rises even on the wicked.

SENECA *De Beneficiis* IV.xxvi.1. Seneca continues, 'The seas lie open even to pirates.' Cf. Matthew v.45: 'He maketh his sun to rise on the evil and on the good, and sendeth rain on the just and on the unjust.'

et seq.
See SEQ.

et sīc dē cēterīs
~ and so too of the rest.

et sīc dē similibus
~ and so too of the like.

et tū, Brūte!
~ You too, Brutus!

The exclamation attributed to Caesar when he saw his supposed friend Brutus among his murderers; see SHAKESPEARE *Julius Caesar* III.i.77.

ēventus stultōrum magister
~ the outcome is the schoolmaster of fools, i.e. anyone can be wise after the event.

LIVY xxii.39. Fabius Maximus says that the successful outcome of his delaying tactics in dealing with Hannibal shows that they are the only way of conducting the war.

ē vestīgiō

~ literally, 'from one's footprint', from where one stands, i.e. instantly, at once.

ex Africā semper aliquid novī

~ always something new from Africa.

A simplification of the original in Pliny's *Natural History* (VIII.xlii.ix): *semper aliquid novī Africam adferre* (Africa always brings [us] something new). This is itself a version of Aristotle's ἀεὶ Λιβύη φέρει τι καινόν (*Historia Animalium* 606b 20). Pliny is here talking about how in Africa animals of different species mate with each other and produce hybrids—hence this common saying of the Greeks.

ex cathedrā

~ with authority.

When the Pope speaks from the papal throne (*cathedra*), he is supposed to speak infallibly. This phrase can be used of any authoritative pronouncement and is often ironical.

excelsior

~ higher.

The motto of the State of New York, adopted by that state on 16 March 1778. In 1841 it was used by Henry Wadsworth Longfellow (1807–82) as an expression of incessant aspiration after higher attainment in a popular poem called 'Excelsior' in which the word is inscribed on the banner carried by a youthful Alpinist: 'A voice replied, far up the height, Excelsior!'

exceptiō probat rēgulam

~ the exception proves the rule.

Attributed by Brewer to COLUMELLA. 'The very fact of exceptions proves that there must be a rule.' Exceptions in fact *test* rules, and if the rules still seem to have force after being tested by exceptions, they are shown to be worthwhile.

exceptīs excipiendīs

~ excepting what is to be excepted; with proper exceptions.

1877 G. ELIOT *Letter* 30 Jan. (1956) VI.335 The cheap edition of my books— which, exceptis excipiendis, is a beautiful edition.

exeat

~ let him her go out.

A permission for temporary absence from English schools and colleges, from monastic houses, etc.

1727–51 CHAMBERS *Cyclopaedia* s.v. His master has given him an exeat.

exēgī monumentum aere perennius
~ I have built a monument more lasting than bronze.

HORACE *Odes* III.xxx.1. The poet proudly emphasizes the durability of his poetry.

exempla sunt odiōsa
~ examples are hateful (or invidious).

examplī grātiā (usually abbreviated to e.g.)
~ for the sake of (or to give) an example.

exeunt omnēs
~ all go out.

A stage direction in plays. Likewise, *exeunt* simply means 'they go out'.

ex grātiā
~ done or given as a favour and not under any compulsion.

ex hypothesī
~ from or according to the hypothesis, as a result of the assumptions made, supposedly, hypothetically.

1603 C. HEYDON *A defence of judiciall astrologie* 211 The Spring and neape tides, the foure seasons of the yere, with infinite like, they are phisically necessarie, they are ineuitable *ex hypothesi*.

exitus ācta probat
~ the outcome justifies the deed.

OVID *Heroides* ii.85. The Latin in fact means not the amoral mistranslation given above, but 'the outcome is the measure of our actions'. However, as a Latin expression divorced from its context, the mistranslation is generally applied.

ex librīs
~ from the library (of).

Commonly inscribed on bookplates.

ex mōre
~ according to custom.

ex nihilō nihil fit

~ out of nothing nothing comes (or is made), i.e. everything must have a cause.

Possibly orginating in the Greek of ALCAEUS (*Fragment* CCCXX), this idea becomes an important concept in the *De Rerum Natura* (On the Nature of the Universe) of the Roman poet Lucretius. Its proverbial ring has given it considerable currency, and not only in Latin.

1551 I. CRANMER *Answer to Gardiner* 369 *Sicut ex nihilo nihil fit, Ita nihil in nihilum redigitur*, As nothyng can been made of nought, so nothynge can be tourned into nought.

Cf. 1605–6 SHAKESPEARE *King Lear* I.i.89 Nothing will come of nothing. Speak again.

ex officiō

~ in discharge of one's duty; in virtue of one's office.

First recorded use in English 1532.

1886 *Oxford University Calendar* 18 The Proctors are *ex-officio* members of each of the under-mentioned Committees.

exoriāre aliquis nostrīs ex ossibus ultor

~ may you arise from my bones, O my unknown avenger!

VIRGIL *Aeneid* iv.625. In a terrifying speech Dido curses Aeneas and his nation. She calls upon the future Carthaginian Hannibal, whose identity she cannot yet know, to take a fearful revenge for Aeneas' abandonment of her.

ex pede Herculem

~ literally, 'Hercules from his foot', i.e. inferring the whole of something from some small or insignificant part of it.

Pythagoras is said by Plutarch to have calculated the height of Hercules from an estimate of the size of his foot. A stadium is 600 feet, but Hercules' stadium at Olympia was much longer. Therefore Hercules's foot was much longer than the average. The foot bears a certain ratio to the height, and so Hercules' height can be ascertained.

expende Hannibalem

~ put Hannibal into the scales.

JUVENAL x.147. The satirist asks what Hannibal's tremendous achievements, which included the crossing of the Alps as well as sensational defeats of Roman armies, in the end amount to. He died an ignominious self-inflicted death. In his famous imitation of this satire, *The Vanity of*

Human Wishes, Samuel Johnson applies Juvenal's message to the career of Charles XII of Sweden (1682–1711) and ends the passage with a fine couplet: 'He left the name, at which the world grew pale, To point a moral, or adorn a tale' (221–2). The idea of weighing a general derives from the Roman bronze steelyard balance. The scale pan hangs from the shorter arm and the counterweight is often the head of a general, which hangs from a loop that is free to move along a graduated scale on the longer arm.

experientia docet stultōs
∼ experience teaches fools.

expertō crēde (or crēdite)
∼ believe one who speaks from experience.

VIRGIL *Aeneid* xi.283. The Greek chieftain Diomedes advises the Italians not to take on the Trojan Aeneas in warfare. He himself knows by his experience in the Trojan War what a great warrior Aeneas is.

1579 s. GOSSON *School of Abuse* f. 17 *Experto crede*, I have seene somewhat, and therefore I thinke I may say the more.

expertus metuit
∼ he who has experienced it is afraid.

HORACE *Epistles* I.xviii.87. The poet warns Lollius of the dangers inherent in cultivating a powerful friend.

ex post factō
∼ from what is done afterward, i.e. after the fact.

This is used of a law made to cover and punish a crime after it has been committed.

ex propriō mōtū
∼ voluntarily.

exstīnctus amābitur īdem
∼ the same man [who was maligned while alive] will be loved when dead.

HORACE *Epistles* II.i.14. Cf. Pope: 'These suns of glory please not till they set.'

ex silentiō
∼ literally, 'from silence'.

The phrase is used to designate an argument or conclusion based on lack of contrary evidence.

1909 L. R. FARNELL *Cults of Greek States* V.iv.88 On this point the argument is not merely *ex silentio*.

ex tempore/extempore

~ without premeditation or preparation; at first sight; off-hand.

1553 N. UDALL *Ralph Roister Doister, A comedy* (Arb.) 32 Yea and extempore will he dities compose.

ex ungue leōnem

~ (judge, or infer) the lion from his claws.

ex ūnō disce omnēs

~ from [the example of] one of them, learn about them all.

This saying is based on VIRGIL *Aeneid* ii.65–6 *crimine ab uno / disce omnes* (from one accusation, learn about all of them), where Aeneas says that one can deduce the treacherous nature of all the Greeks from the fraudulent Sinon.

ex vōtō

~ according to one's vow or prayer.

faber est quisque fortūnae suae
~ every man is the architect of his own fortune.

A proverb quoted by SALLUST (?) *De Republica* i.2.

faciēs nōn omnibus ūna
~ all do not look alike.

facile prīnceps
~ (a person who is) easily first; the acknowledged leader or chief.

1834 GREVILLE *The Greville memoirs* (1874) III.xxii.64 In the prime of life, . . . *facile princeps* in the House of Commons.

facilis dēscēnsus Avernī
~ the descent by Avernus is easy.

VIRGIL *Aeneid* vi.126. The Sibyl tells Aeneas that it is easy to go down to the underworld; the problem lies in returning. This quotation is more generally applied to mean that it is easy to slip into evil ways.

facit indignātiō versum
~ indignation makes verse.

JUVENAL i.79. The satirist is prompted to write by a sense of outrage. The epitaph on the great Irish satirist Jonathan Swift (1667–1745) expresses the hope that he is now at last resting 'where savage indignation can no longer tear his heart'. Cf. UBI SAEVA INDIGNATIO ULTERIUS COR LACERARE NEQUIT.

facta, nōn verba
~ deeds, not words.

factum est
~ it is done.

fācundī calicēs quem nōn fēcēre disertum?
  See FĒCUNDĪ CALICĒS ...

faex populī
  ∼ the dregs of the people.

falsus in ūnō, falsus in omnibus
  ∼ false in one point, false in all.

fāma clāmōsa
  ∼ a noisy rumour; current scandal.

fāma crēscit eundō
  ∼ rumour gathers strength as it goes.

  Cf. VIRGIL *Aeneid* iv.174–5. The personification of rumour spreads the news
  of the love affair between Dido and Aeneas, with devastating results.
  Virgil is here making use of Lucretius' concept of CRESCIT EUNDO.

fāmā nihil est celerius
  ∼ nothing is swifter than rumour.

  In Virgil's *Aeneid*, Fama (Rumour) is described; though not in these exact
  words, as being unsurpassed by any evil thing in speed (iv.174).

fāma semper vīvat!
  ∼ may his/her fame live for ever!

fās est et ab hoste docērī
  ∼ it is right to learn a lesson even from an enemy.

  OVID *Metamorphoses* iv.428.

fāta obstant
  ∼ the Fates block the way.

  VIRGIL *Aeneid* iv.440. Aeneas cannot yield to Dido's pleas. Fate has another
  destiny for him which shuts him off from her.

fāta viam invenient
  ∼ the Fates will find a way.

  VIRGIL *Aeneid* x.113. Jupiter says that he will play no part in the fighting
  between the Italians and the Trojans. Fate will have to find its own way
  without help from him.

favēte linguīs
  ∼ keep a religious silence.

HORACE *Odes* III.i.2. The expression literally means 'be favourable with your tongues', i.e. 'avoid words of bad omen'. The best way to do that is to keep silent.

fēcit
~ made by.

On a work of art, generally followed by the artist's name.

fēcundī (or fācundī) calicēs quem nōn fēcēre disertum?
~ whom have not life-giving (*or* eloquent) cups made ready of speech?

HORACE *Epistles* I.v.19. Horace celebrates the stimulating power of wine.

fēlīcitās multōs habet amīcōs
~ good fortune has many friends.

fēlīx culpa
~ literally, 'happy fault', referring to the Fall of Man or the sin of Adam as resulting in the blessedness of the Redemption; thus an apparent error or tragedy which has happy consequences.

1913 *Maclean's Magazine* Oct. 42/2 Shall we call it a *culpa felix* that brought you to me?

1986 *Time* 10 Nov. 25/1 He was crushed in a landslide of historic proportions. Today he sees it as a kind of *felix culpa*, a happy fall.

fēlīx quī potuit rērum cognōscere causās
~ happy the man who was able to discover the causes of things.

VIRGIL *Georgics* ii.490. Virgil here celebrates his great predecessor Lucretius, whose astonishing philosophical poem *De Rerum Natura* (On the Nature of the Universe) sought to banish superstitious beliefs.

ferē libenter hominēs id quod volunt crēdunt
~ people are generally glad to believe that what they want to be true is so.

CAESAR *De Bello Gallico* III.xviii.7.

fervet opus
~ the work seethes.

VIRGIL *Aeneid* i.436. As Aeneas observes the construction of the city of Carthage, he sees the builders working in a happily cooperative spirit like bees. Everywhere he looks is seething with activity.

festīnā lentē
∼ make haste slowly.

This is a Latin version of a Greek motto of Augustus (SUETONIUS *Augustus* xxv.4), who linked solid achievement with caution.

1590 T. LODGE *Rosalynde* (1592) sig. O2r *Festina lenter* [*sic*], especially in loue.

fīat
∼ let it be done, i.e. an authoritative pronouncement, decree or order.

First recorded use in English 1636.

1883 J. HAWTHORNE *Dust* I.44 Whose fiat in matters of fashion was law.

fīat experimentum in corpore vīlī
∼ let experiment be made on a worthless body.

A sinister medical recommendation. Cf. CORPUS VILE.

fīat iūstitia et pereat mundus
∼ let justice be done, though the world perish.

The motto of Emperor Ferdinand I (1503–64).

1563 J. MANLIUS *Locorum Communium Collectanea* II.290.

fīat iūstitia et ruant coelī
∼ let justice be done, even though the heavens fall.

This is the version given in the first citation in English of the famous maxim in the previous entry. It is from William Watson's *A Decacordon of Ten Quodlibetical Questions Concerning Religion and State* (1602).

fīat lūx
∼ let there be light.

Genesis i.3 in the Vulgate (the Latin translation of the Bible). Part of the biblical myth of creation.

1680 S. CHARNOCK *Several discourses of the existence and attributes of God* in *Works*. (1684) II.405 The new Creation as well as the old begins with a *Fiat lux*.

fideī dēfēnsor
∼ defender of the faith.

In 1521 Pope Leo X gave Henry VIII of England this title for having written a work defending the Seven Sacraments against Luther, the German reformer. He and all succeeding English monarchs have hung on to this appellation, despite Henry's split with the Church of Rome in the 1530s. The title is abbreviated to **FD** on British coins.

fidem qui perdit, nihil pote ultrā perdere
~ the man who loses his honour can lose nothing further.

PUBLILIUS SYRUS *Sententiae* F.14.

fīde, sed cui vīdē
~ trust, but be careful in whom.

fides Pūnica
~ 'Punic faith', i.e. treachery.

The Poeni (Carthaginians) were regarded by the Romans as peculiarly treacherous. Livy relates (XXII.vi.11–12) how after the battle of Lake Trasimene (217 BC), when the Carthaginian cavalry commander Maharbal promised the Romans that he would let them go if they surrendered, Hannibal threw them into chains: thus, as Livy remarks with biting sarcasm, Maharbal's pledge (*fides*) was observed with Punic reverence (*Punica religione*). *See also* PUNICA FIDES.

fīdus Achātes
~ faithful Achates, i.e. a devoted follower or henchman.

VIRGIL *Aeneid* vi.158, etc. Achates is Aeneas' somewhat nondescript companion in Virgil's poem.

1603 C. HEYDON *An astrological discourse in justification of the validity of astrology* XX.411 Yet I haue tied my selfe to be *fidus Achates* to him.

fīliōque
~ 'and from the Son'.

The word inserted in the version of the Nicene Creed used by the Western Church to assert the doctrine of the procession of the Holy Spirit from the Son as well as from the Father, which is not admitted in the Eastern Church.

1876 C. M. DAVIES *Unorthodox London* 90 With reference to the 'Filioque' clause, 'One branch of the Church Catholic affirms on this point, whilst the other declines to affirm'.

fīlius nūllius
~ a son of nobody; a bastard.

fīlius terrae
~ a son of the earth; a low-born person.

fīnem laudā

~ literally, 'praise the end', i.e. if things work out successfully, then is the time to applaud.

fīnem respice

~ look to the end.

fīnis

~ the end.

This word was formerly—and is still occasionally—put at the end of a book. Richard Brinsley Sheridan scrawled it at the end of the long-delayed manuscript of *The School for Scandal* (1777). Beneath it he added 'Thank God! RBS'.

fīnis corōnat opus

~ the end crowns the work.

A celebration of the completion of a work.

flagrante dēlictō

~ in the commission of the crime; in the very act.

Cf. 1832 E. W. ROBERTSON *Historical essays in connexion with the land and the church* 137 When an offender was taken in flagrant delict.

flamma fūmō est proxima

~ literally, 'flame is very close to smoke', i.e. there's no smoke without fire.

PLAUTUS *Curculio* 53.

flectere sī nequeō superōs, Acheronta movēbō

~ if I cannot move the gods, I shall stir up hell.

VIRGIL *Aeneid* vii.312. Juno will stop at nothing to obstruct the mission of Aeneas and his Trojan refugees.

flectī, nōn frangī

~ to be bent, not to be broken.

flōreat Etōna

~ may Eton flourish.

The motto of Eton College.

1888 C. A. WILKINSON *Reminiscences of Eton* xxxiv.340 Join with one heart and voice in the old shout, 'Floreat Etona'.

flōruit (abbreviated is fl.)

~ literally, 'he/she flourished.'

The word is used to refer to refer to the period during which a person's career was at its height.

1843 LIDDELL & SCOTT *Greek-English Dictionary* Preface The date of each Author's 'floruit' is added in the margin.

fōns et orīgō

~ the souce and origin (of).

First recorded use in English 1809.

1873 R. BROWNING *Red cotton night-cap country* iii.202 Never mind the cause, *Fons et origo* of the malady: Apply the drug with courage!

forsan et haec ōlim meminisse iuvābit

~ perhaps one day it will give us pleasure to recall even these things.

VIRGIL *Aeneid* i.203. Aeneas tries to encourage his men by saying that the adventures they have endured, however horrific to experience, may yet give them pleasure to look back on.

fortēs fortūna adiuvat

~ fortune favours the brave.

TERENCE *Phormio* I.iv.26. This is just one formulation of a sentiment found in Ennius (*Annals* 257) and Virgil (*Aeneid* x.284). The Terence motto was quoted by Pliny the Elder when he decided to go ahead with his rescue mission during the eruption of Vesuvius in AD 79 (PLINY *Letters* VI.xvi.11). Chancer has an early (*c.* 1385) instance of the sentiment in his *Troilus & Criseyde* (iv.600). 'Thenk ek Fortune, as wel thiselves woost, Helpeth hardy man to his enprise.'

fortiter in rē, suāviter in modō

~ forcibly in deed, gently in manner.

Based on C. AQUAVIVA *Industriae ad curandos animae morbos* (1606) ii.1.

fortūnātī ambō!

~ you happy pair!

VIRGIL *Aeneid* ix.446. The poet celebrates the homosexual lovers Nisus and Euryalus who have met their deaths fighting for the Trojan cause. They are happy in that their memory, according to Virgil, will last as long as Jupiter's Rome.

fortūna vitrea est: tum cum splendet frangitur
～ fortune is made of glass: at the moment when it is shining, it shatters.

PUBLILIUS SYRUS *Sententiae* F.24.

frangās, nōn flectēs
～ you may break, you shall not bend me.

frontī nūlla fides
～ no reliance on the face, i.e. no trusting appearances.

JUVENAL ii.8. Juvenal denounces those who preach morality but have no morals.

fugācēs lābuntur annī
See EHEU! FUGACES LABUNTUR ANNI.

fugit hōra
～ the hour flies.

PERSIUS v.153. A personification of Luxury gives the standard Epicurean advice: 'time flies, death looms'. Cf. CARPE DIEM.

fugit irreparābile tempus
～ irrecoverable time flies on.

VIRGIL *Georgics* iii.285. Virgil, in his great poem about farming, says that, since time is moving on, he must stop talking about the care of herds and move on to sheep and goats. Yet this quotation can be taken as another Epicurean statement of the speedy and irreversible passage of time. Cf. FUGIT HORA.

fuimus Troes
～ we were once Trojans.

VIRGIL *Aeneid* ii.325. On the night of the sack of Troy, the priest Panthus gives voice to the realization that Troy is now finished; their days as Trojans are over.

fuit llium
～ llium (Troy) has been, i.e. Troy is no more.

VIRGIL *Aeneid* ii.325. These are Panthus' next words after FUIMUS TROES. At the end of the seventeenth century (1693–97), John Dryden translated these two statements: 'Troy is no more, and llium was a town.'

fulmen brūtum
~ a harmless thunderbolt; a vain threat.

Cf. BRUTUM FULMEN.

furor arma ministrat
~ frenzy finds arms for them.

VIRGIL *Aeneid* i.150. The poet pictures a mob rioting, and seizing anything which might serve as an offensive weapon. The emotion of *furor* is viewed as highly dangerous—and highly combustible—in the *Aeneid*, and in Roman thought generally.

furor Teutonicus
~ Teutonic frenzy.

Based on LUCAN *Pharsalia* i.255–6, where the inhabitants of the Italian town of Rimini reflect on their disastrous location. They were the key city between Gaul and Italy, controlling the bottle-neck between Apennines and Adriatic. They had thus been exposed to the frenzy of the Teutons, a Germanic tribe, at the end of the second century BC. In fact the Teutons were annihilated by Caius Marius in the battle of Aquae Sextiae (Aix-en-Provence) in 102 BC.

Gallia est omnis dīvīsa in partēs trēs
∼ Gaul, viewed as a whole, is divided into three parts.

The famous opening words of Caesar's *De Bello Gallico* (I.i.1).

gaudeāmus igitur
∼ so let us be joyful.

The opening words of a German student song (which continues *iuvenes dum sumus* (while we are young)). The expression can also be used to refer to a college-students' merry-making.

1823 W. SCOTT *Familiar Letters* (1894) II.178 Our Bannatyne Club goes on *à merveille*, only that at our *gaudeamus* this year we drank our wine *more majorum*, and our new judge Lord Eldin had a bad fall on the staircase.

gaudet tentāmine virtūs
∼ virtue rejoices in being tested.

genius locī
∼ the spirit or guardian deity of the place.

1771 SMOLLET *The expedition of Humphry Clinker*—To Dr. Lewis 8 Aug. The pleasure-grounds are, in my opinion, not so well laid out according to the *genius loci*.

gēns togāta
∼ the nation which wore the toga, i.e. the Romans.

Virgil insists on this proud accoutrement of the Roman race—a highly unsuitable garment for so hot a climate—at *Aeneid* i.282.

genus irrītābile vātum
∼ the irritable tribe of poets.

HORACE *Epistles* II.ii.102. Horace says that while he was writing, he felt obliged to join in a mutual admiration society with captious fellow poets, but now he has had enough of this.

Geōrgium sīdus

~ one of the greater planets, now called Uranus, so named by its discoverer, Sir William Herschel, in honour of George III.

gignī de nihilō nihilum, in nihilum nīl posse revertī

~ from nothing nothing can come, into nothing nothing can return.

PERSIUS iii.84. The satirical poet makes the point that most people mock the Epicureans who are concerned with this sort of subject. *See* DE NIHILO NIHILUM, IN NIHILUM NIL POSSE REVERTI.

glōria

~ glory.

A title of certain doxologies beginning with this word, as in *gloria in excelsis Deo* (glory to God in the highest), the words of Luke ii.14.

gradus ad Parnassum

~ a step, or stairs, to Parnassus (the mountain where the Muses dwelt); a Latin or Greek poetical dictionary.

The *Gradus* gave the 'quantities' of words and suggested poetical epithets and phraseology. The earliest edition of the *Gradus* in the British Museum was published in Cologne in 1687; there was a London edition in 1691.

1764 R. LLOYD *Poetry Professors* 6 What reams of paper will be spoil'd! What graduses be daily soil'd By inky fingers, greasy thumbs, Hunting the word that never comes!

Graecia capta ferum victōrem cēpit et artēs intulit agrestī Latiō

~ Greece, once overcome, overcame her wild conqueror, and brought the arts into rustic Latium.

HORACE *Epistles* II.i.156–7. The poet is making the point that, though Rome conquered Greece militarily, she owed almost all her literature, and her arts generally, to Greek models. Latium was an area in central Italy.

Graeculus ēsuriēns

~ the hungry Greekling.

JUVENAL iii.78. The racist poet talks with scorn of the infinitely adaptable Greeks who in his view pollute Rome: 'All sciences a fasting monsieur knows, And bid him go to Hell, to Hell he goes!' (from Samuel Johnson's *London* (1738), his imitation of Juvenal's third satire).

grammaticī certant

∼ grammarians fight it out.

HORACE *Ars Poetica* 78. The poet talks scornfully of scholarly pedantry.

grātīs anhēlāns, multa agendō nihil agēns

∼ out of breath to no purpose and achieving nothing by frantic activity.

PHAEDRUS *Fabulae Aesopiae* II.v.3. Phaedrus talks about the busybodies at Rome. Cf. Chaucer (General Prologue to the *Canterbury Tales* 323–4) on his Sergeant of the Lawe: 'Nowher so bisy a man as he ther nas, And yet he semed bisier than he was.'

graviōra manent

∼ greater dangers await (you).

VIRGIL *Aeneid* vi.84. The Sibyl at Cumae in south Italy tells Aeneas that, though he has undergone great perils at sea, still greater dangers are in store for him on land.

gutta cavat lapidem

∼ the drop wears away the stone.

OVID *Ex Ponto* IV.x.5. In his exile Ovid complains that while stones are worn away, he himself lives on.

habeās corpus

~ you (i.e. the accuser) are to produce the body.

The main provision of the Habeas Corpus Act, which dates from 1679, is the requiremeànt that the body of a person restrained of liberty should be brought before the judge or into court so that the lawfulness of the restraint may be investigated and determined.

habēmus Papam

~ we have a Pope.

The formula with which the election of a new Pope is announced.

habent sua fāta libellī

~ books have their destinies.

MAURUS *De litteris, syllabis et metris* 1286. Each book sets out on a journey of its own to meet a reception which cannot be foreknown. Near the end of *Troïlus & Criseyde* Chaucer writes, 'Go, litel bok, go, litel myn tragedye . . .' (v.1786).

hāc lēge

~ with this law, under this condition.

haec ōlim meminisse iuvābit

See FORSAN ET HAEC OLIM MEMINISSE IUVABIT.

hanc veniam petimusque damusque vicissim

~ this freedom we (poets) ask and grant in turn.

HORACE *Ars Poetica* 11. The freedom referred to is the time-honoured privilege of unlimited audacity in invention.

Hannibal ad portās

~ Hannibal at the gates.

CICERO *Philippic* I.v.11. Cicero is complaining that Antony tried to force him to attend a meeting of the Senate. Was it a real emergency—such as Hannibal, Rome's deadly Carthaginian enemy, at the city gates? No.

haud ignōta loquor

~ I say things that are not unknown.

VIRGIL *Aeneid* ii.91.

hēlluō librōrum

~ glutton of books, an out-and-out bookworm; someone who gorges himself or herself on books.

heu pietās! heu prīsca fidēs!

~ alas for his piety! alas for his old-world loyalty!

VIRGIL *Aeneid* vi.878. The ghost of Anchises, Aeneas' father, laments with infinite sadness the fate of the young Marcellus, the nephew and son-in-law of Augustus, who died in 23 BC. His wonderful qualities proved no defence against death.

hiātus valdē dēflendus

~ a gap greatly to be lamented.

hīc et nunc

~ at the present time and place, in this particular situation.

1935 *Studies in History of Ideas* III.469   One must distinguish between the *type* or *kind* of a sign, and its *hic et nunc*, spatio-temporal exemplification.

hīc iacet

~ here lies.

Inscribed on tombstones followed by the name of the dead person.

hinc illae lacrimae

~ hence these tears, i.e. there is the true grievance.

TERENCE *Andria* I.i.126. This proverbial expression was used by Cicero (*Pro Caelio* xxv.61) and Horace (*Epistles* I.xix.41).

hinc lūcem et pōcula sacra

~ from this source (come) light and draughts of sacred learning.

The motto of Cambridge University. It was first used by the University Printer in 1603, accompanied by an engraving of the Cambridge emblem, an allegorical figure of 'kind mother Cambridge' (*alma mater Cantabrigia*) whose naked breasts flow with the milk of sound learning and piety. In one hand she holds the sun of revealed truth, in the other a cup into which the blessings of heaven pour. The image of Cambridge as a fertile woman soon became well known. In a poem published in 1662, Michael Drayton addressed his 'most beloved Towne' of Cambridge thus:

> The woman's perfect shape, still be thy emblem right,
> Whose one hand holds a cup, the other bears a light.

No source for the motto has been discovered. It was probably composed as part of the emblem.

hoc erat in vōtis
~ this was among my prayers.

HORACE *Satires* II.vi.1. The poet is thrilled at the farm in the Sabine hills which his patron Maecenas has given him.

hoc genus omne
See ET HOC GENUS OMNE.

hoc opus, hic labor est
~ this is the difficulty, this is the trouble.

VIRGIL *Aeneid* vi.129. The Sibyl tells Aeneas that it is easy to go down to the underworld (*see* FACILIS DESCENSUS AVERNI); it's getting back up to the upper world that is the problem.

hoc volo, sīc iubeō, sit prō ratiōne voluntās
~ this is my will and my command: let my will stand as a reason.

JUVENAL vi.223. Juvenal conjures up a devastating picture of a tyrannical wife, here insisting that her husband crucifies a slave who has done nothing wrong. Cf. Shakespeare, *Julius Ceasar* II.ii.71: 'The cause is in my will, I will not come.'

hominis est errāre
~ it is human to err.

homō antīquā virtūte et fidē
~ a man of old-fashioned virtue and loyalty.

TERENCE *Adelphi* III.iii.88.

homō est sociāle animal
~ man is a social animal, i.e. not intended to live alone.

Based on SENECA *De Clementia* I.iii.2.

homō hominī lupus

~ man is a wolf to man.

Based on PLAUTUS *Asinaria* 495. A summation of man's inhumanity to man. *See* LUPUS EST HOMO HOMINI for a fuller comment.

homō nūllius colōris

~ a man of no colour, a man who does not commit himself.

homō sum; hūmānī nihil ā mē aliēnum putō

~ I am a man and think that there is no human problem which does not concern me.

TERENCE *Heauton Timorumenos* (The Self-Tormentor) I.i.25. This noble sentiment is tucked away in a little-known Roman comedy.

honesta mors turpī vītā potior

~ an honourable death is preferable to a shameful life.

The Stoic Roman chose to commit suicide rather than to live on in shameful circumstances.

honōris causā

~ literally, 'for the sake of honour', i.e. honorary.

Now used chiefly as a description of such university degrees as are conferred upon persons in recognition of certain distinctions or achievements without the customary academic examination or thesis.

honor virtūtis praemium

~ honour is the reward of virtue.

honōs alit artēs

~ honour nourishes the arts.

CICERO *Tusculan Disputations* I.ii.4. The fact that the arts are honoured and praised is a great incentive to artists.

hōra fugit

~ the hour flies, time passes.

hōrās nōn numerō nisi serēnās

~ I number only (literally, 'none but') shining hours.

An inscription common on sundials.

horrēscō referēns

~ I shudder as I relate.

VIRGIL *Aeneid* ii.204. Aeneas shudders as he tells of the two huge snakes sent by the gods over the sea to kill Laocoon, the priest of Neptune, and his sons. Laocoon does not wish the wooden horse to be taken into Troy and has in fact thrown a spear at it, but fate had determined that Troy must fall and so Laocoon has to be destroyed.

horribile dictū
~ horrible to relate.

1854 G. ELIOT in *Westminster Review* Oct. 467   In some circles the effort is, who shall make the best puns, *(horrible dictu!)* or the best charades.

horror vacuī
~ dread of emptiness, i.e. the dislike of leaving empty spaces, e.g. in an artistic composition.

1845 W. PLATE *Ptolemy's Knowledge of Arabia* 5   Ptolemy had a tendency towards putting the inland towns too far east; but whether it was a mere *horror vacui*, or some misunderstanding, that induced him to do so, cannot be decided.

hūmānum est errāre
~ to err is human.

hunc tū cavētō
~ beware of this man.

hypothesēs nōn fingō
~ I do not frame hypotheses (i.e. unverifiable speculations).

Isaac Newton (1642–1727).

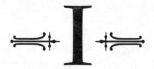

ibidem (abreviated to **ibid.** or **ib.**)

   ~ in the same place, i.e. in the same book, chapter, passage, etc.

Used to avoid the repetition of a reference. First recorded use in English 1663.

idem sonāns

   ~ identity of sound in pronunciation, the occurrence in a document of a word or name misspelt but having the sound of the word or name intended.

1843 WHARTON *Law Lexicon* 304/2 The courts will not interfere in setting aside proceedings on account of the misspelling of names, provided . . . there is an *idem sonans* between the pronunciation of the right name and that which is inserted in the proceedings; as Lawrance, instead of Lawrence, Reynell for Reynolds, Beniditto for Benedetto.

idem velle atque idem nōlle ea dēmum firma amīcitia est

   ~ to like and to dislike the same things is indeed true friendship.

SALLUST *Bellum Catilinae* 20.

id est (usually abbreviated to **i.e.**)

   ~ that is (to say).

Used to introduce an explanation of a word or phrase.

1598 FLORIO *Worlde of Wordes* *Gallina bagnata*, a wet hen, id est, a milke sop.

id genus omne

   ~ all that class, all of that sort.

See ET HOC GENUS OMNE.

Iēsus Nazarēnus Rēx Iūdaeōrum

   ~ Jesus of Nazareth, King of the Jews.

The mocking words set on the cross above the crucified Jesus (Matthew xxvii.37). In paintings of the Crucifixion they are usually abbreviated to INRI.

ignis aurum probat, miseria fortēs virōs
~ fire tests gold, suffering tests brave men.

SENECA *De Providentia* v.9. Our behaviour in adversity is the test of our courage.

ignis fatuus
~ literally, 'foolish fire', a phosphorescent light seen hovering or flitting over marshy ground, and supposed to be due to the spontaneous combustion of an inflammable gas (methane) derived from decaying organic matter.

Popular names for the phenomenon include 'will-o'-the-wisp' and 'Jack-o'-lantern'. The term is commonly used to describe any delusive guiding principle, hope or aim.

1563 W. FULKE *Meteors* (1640) 11b This impression seene on the land, is called in Latine, *ignis fatuus*, foolish fire, that hurteth not, but only feareth fooles.

ignōrantia lēgis nēminem excūsat
~ ignorance of the law excuses no one (i.e. is no excuse).

ignōtī nūlla cupīdō
~ literally, 'no desire for the unknown', i.e. what the eye doesn't see the heart doesn't long for.

ignōtum per ignōtius
~ the unknown by means of the more unknown, i.e. an explanation which is harder to understand than what it is meant to explain.

1386 CHAUCER *Canon's Yeoman's Tale* 1457:

And Plato answerde unto hym anoon,
'Take the stoon that Titanos men name.'
'Which is that' quod he. 'Magnasia is the same,'
Seyde Plato, 'Ye, sire, and it is thus?
This [is] *ignotum per ignocius* [i.e. *ignotius*].
What is Magnasia, good sire, I yow preye?'

Ilias malōrum
~ literally, 'an Iliad of evils', i.e. a sea of troubles.

CICERO *Ad Atticum* viii.11. Homer's great epic poem, the *Iliad*, runs the gamut of human suffering. Thomas de Quincey wrote of 'an Iliad of woes' in his *Confessions of an English Opium-Eater*.

ille crucem sceleris pretium tulit, hic diadēma

∿ that man got a cross, this man a crown, as the price of his crime.

JUVENAL xiii.105.

immortālia nē spērēs

∿ so that you may not hope to be immortal.

HORACE *Odes* IV.vii.7. Horace tells Torquatus that the cycle of the year should warn him not to hope that his life will go on for ever.

īmō pectore *See* AB IMO PECTORE.

impār congressus Achillī

∿ literally, 'unequal in conflict with Achilles', i.e. no match for the greatest of warriors.

VIRGIL *Aeneid* i.475. Virgil here refers to the episode in the Trojan War when the Trojan Troilus flees in vain from the mighty Achilles.

imparī Marte

∿ literally, 'with Mars [the god of war] unequal', i.e. with unequal military strength.

imperium

∿ command, absolute power.

1651 T. GOODWIN *Works*. (1862) IV.144 All the operations of all the powers in it are immediately and entirely at the arbitrary *imperium* and dominion of the soul.

imprimātur

∿ literally, 'let it be printed'.

This is generally used of a commendatory licence or sanction.

1672 A. MARVELL *Rehearsal Transprosed* i.46 As things of Buffoonery do commonly, they carry with them their own *imprimatur*.

imprīmīs

∿ literally, 'among the first things', i.e. in the first place, first.

First recorded use in English 1465.

1700 W. CONGREVE *Way of World* IV.v. in *Works*. 278/1 *Imprimis* then, I covenant, that your acquaintance be general.

improbe Amor, quid nōn mortālia pectora cōgis?

∼ cruel love, to what extremes do you not drive our human hearts?

VIRGIL *Aeneid* iv.412. Virgil cries out in sympathy for Dido, the unhappy queen of Carthage whose lover Aeneas has abandoned her. At this point in the tragic story, she is about to send her sister Anna down to the harbour to plead with him not to sail away. Inevitably it proves a futile mission.

in absentiā

∼ in his/her/their absence.

Used most commonly of those who are not present in person when they receive a university degree or are convicted or cleared of a crime.

1886 *Edinburgh University Calendar 1885/6* 141 Conferred *in absentia*.

in āctū

∼ in practice (as opposed to theory or potentiality).

First recorded use in English 1680.

1907 W. JAMES *Pragmatism* vi.222 Health *in actu* means, among other things, good sleeping and digesting.

in aeternum

∼ for eternity, for ever.

in antīs

∼ with pillars on each side of the doors.

This architectural term denotes a building in which the side walls are prolonged beyond the front and the pillars terminating them are in line with the columns of the facade.

First recorded use in English 1848.

1973 *Country Life* 20 Sept. 763/3 Its original first-floor portico, with Ionic columns *in antis*, survives.

in articulō mortis

∼ at the point or moment of death.

The last words of a dying person carry especial weight in law since they are thought likely to be truthful. The assumption is that generally at that stage nothing is to be gained by lying.

in bancō

∼ literally, 'on the bench'.

The phrase is applied to sittings of a Superior Court of Common Law as a full court.

in bellō parvīs mōmentīs magnī casūs intercēdunt

~ in war great events are the result of trivial causes.

Based on CAESAR *De Bello Civili* I.xxi.2.

in camerā

~ literally, 'in an arched or vaulted chamber', e.g. in a judge's private chambers, not in open court or, more generally, in secret or private session, not in public. The Latin word *camera* is used (in its sense of a vaulted chamber), without the *in*, of the Camera of the Radcliffe Library at Oxford (the Radcliffe Camera).

in capite

~ in chief.

First recorded use in English 1558.

1767 BLACKSTONE *Commentaries on the Laws of England* II.60 All tenures being thus derived . . . from the king, those that held immediately under him . . . were called his tenants in capite, or in chief.

in caudā venēnum

~ the poison (is) in the tail.

Just as the scorpion's sting is in its tail, so we should look beyond first impressions and guard against a lurking peril which could await us. Bland smiles may be followed by a vicious onslaught.

incidis in Scyllam cupiēns vītāre Charybdim

~ literally, 'you meet with Scylla in your desire to avoid Charybdis', i.e. out of the frying pan into the fire.

On either side of the Straits of Messina between Italy and Sicily were Charybdis, a whirlpool which sucked all that tried to cross it into its depths, and Scylla, a ghastly female monster living on a rock who snatched up passing mariners with her tentacles in order to devour them (*Odyssey* xii). The meaning of the expression is that in avoiding one danger, one must be careful not to fall into another.

incipit

~ (here) beginneth.

Used by medieval scribes in indicating the beginning of a new treatise or poem or a division in a Latin or sometimes English manuscript.

1377 LANGLAND *Piers Ploroman* B Incipit liber de Petro Plowman (here beginneth the book concerning Piers Plowman).

1973 *Times* 2 Nov. 6/1 The *incipits*, or titular opening phrases, of more than 200 literary works current in Sumer in the early second millennium B.C.

incrēdulus ōdī
∿ I hate it because I do not believe it.

HORACE *Ars Poetica* 188. The poet says that it is better to keep horrific or miraculous events off the stage. If he actually sees Medea killing her children or Cadmus turning into a snake rather than hearing these events described, he does not believe them and therefore is simply repelled.

index expūrgatōrius
∿ expurgated list.

See next entry.

index librōrum prohibitōrum
∿ list of forbidden books.

This list is of books which Roman Catholics are forbidden to read, or may read only in expurgated editions. With regard to the latter, the portions to be deleted or altered are sometimes indicated in an *Index expurgatorius* (list of expurgations).

1613 S. PURCHAS *Pilgrimage* (1614) 90 L. Vives ... when he telleth tales out of Schoole, the good mans tongue is shortned, and their Index purgeth out that wherewith hee seeketh to purge their leaven.

in distāns
∿ at a distance.

1890 W. JAMES *The principles of psychology* I.ii.47 This blindness was probably due to inhibitions exerted *in distans*.

in dubiō
∿ in doubt.

indignor quandōque bonus dormitat Homērus
∿ I feel agrieved when the good Homer nods.

HORACE *Ars Poetica* 359. The poet laments that even the best of poets has his bad moments.

in esse
∿ in (actual) existence.

After a child is born it is *in esse*; before it is born it is IN POSSE.

inest clēmentia fortī
∿ mercy is natural to a brave man.

in excelsīs

~ in the highest (places), i.e. in heaven. *See also under* GLORIA.

in extēnsō

~ at full length.

1826 *Congress Debates* II.ii.1767 It might not suit the views of the Government, to give, *in extenso*, the instructions given to our Ministers.

in extrēmīs

~ in the last agonies, at the very point of death.

1530 R. PACE *Letter to Wolsey* in Ellis *Original Letters* ser. iii I.199 Mr. Dean off Paulis hath Iyen continually synst Thursdaye *in extremis* and is not yitt dedde.

infandum, rēgīna, iubēs renovāre dolōrem

~ You bid me, o queen, to renew an unspeakable grief.

VIRGIL *Aeneid* ii.3. Dido has asked Aeneas to tell her the story of the sack of his city of Troy and the journey which has led him to Carthage where she is queen. With this declaration of reluctance, he launches into his tale.

īnfima speciēs

~ the lowest species of a classification.

1645 J. HOWELL *Letters* I.xii.23 Being contented to be the *infima species*, the lowest in the predicament of your friends.

in fīne

~ literally, 'at the end', i.e. finally, in short, to sum up.

in flagrante dēlictō *See* FLAGRANTE DELICTO.

in fōrmā pauperis

~ in the form or guise of a poor person (exempted from liability to pay the costs of an action); hence, in a humble or abject manner.

1592 R. GREENE *Quip for Upstart Courtier* E j b The poore man that ... pleads in *forma pauperis*.

īnfrā

~ below, underneath; further on in a book or article.

The pages after the one you are reading are under it.

1888 *Encyclopaedia Britannica* XXVIII.702/1 *See infra* in regard to rotary printing.

īnfrā dignitātem (often abbreviated to **infra dig.**)
  ∼ beneath one's dignity, unbecoming one's position, not consistent with dignity, undignified.

1822 W. HAZLITT *Table-talk* (1885) 287 If the graduates . . . express their thoughts in English, it is understood to be *infra dignitatem*.

in futūrō
  ∼ in the future.

in gremiō lēgis
  ∼ literally, 'in the bosom of the law', i.e. under the protection of the law.

inhūmānum verbum est ultiō
  ∼ revenge is an inhuman word.

SENECA *Dialogi* IV.xxxii.1.

in īnfīnītum
  ∼ to infinity, without end.

See AD INFINITUM.

1564 E. GRINDAL *Funeral Sermon on the Emperor Ferdinand* in *Remains* (1843) And so *in infinitum*, until all years and days be clean past and expired.

iniūriārum remedium est oblīviō
  ∼ the best remedy for injuries is to forget them.

PUBLILIUS SYRUS *Sententiae* I.21.

in līmine
  ∼ on the threshold, at the very outset.

1804 *Edinburgh Review* July 297 One objection, *in limine*, we feel ourselves called upon to make.

in locō
  ∼ literally, 'in the place', i.e. in the right or proper place, spot, or situation.

See also DESIPERE IN LOCO.

in locō parentis
  ∼ in the place or position of a parent.

First recorded use in English 1710.

1828 *Congress Debates* IV.i.1335 I now stand to them, *in loco parentis*, in the place of a father.

in magnīs et voluisse sat est
∿ in great affairs, it is enough to have the will.

PROPERTIUS II.x.6. The love poet says that he is thinking of writing a martial epic, and if his powers fall short, surely his boldness will be praised.

in mediās rēs
∿ into the midst of affairs; into the middle of a narrative.

1786 H. MORE *Bas Bleu* 33 But be as epic as I please, And plunge at once in medias res.

in mediō tūtissimus ībis
∿ you will go most safely in the middle course.

Based on OVID *Metamorphoses* ii.137. The sun god recommends the middle course to his son Phaethon as the latter is on the point of driving the former's chariot through the sky, with disastrous results.

in memoriam
∿ to the memory of, in memory of.

Common as the beginning of an epitaph or commemorative inscription.
1850 TENNYSON (title) In Memoriam A. H. H. Obiit MDCCCXXXIII.

in nōmine Patris et Fīliī et Spīritūs Sānctī
∿ in the name of the Father and of the Son and of the Holy Spirit.

in nūbibus
∿ literally, 'in the clouds', i.e. not yet settled or decided; also, incapable of being carried out.

1583 BABINGTON *A very fruitful exposition of the Commandments* To Gentl. Glamorgan, Both the fee and freehold of the Church is in suspence, and *in nubibus*.

in nuce
∿ in a nutshell, in a condensed form.

1854 G. ELIOT tr. Feuerbach's *Essence of Christianity* II.xxii.214 The religious man is happy in his imagination; he has all things *in nuce*; his possessions are always portable.

in omnia parātus
∿ ready for everything.

inopem mē cōpia fēcit
∿ abundance has made me poor.

Ovid here (*Metamorphoses* iii.466) shows us Narcissus gazing lovingly at his reflection in the water. He has everything he wants, and yet because he cannot have himself, he feels that he has nothing.

in ovō

~ literally, 'in the egg', i.e. in embryo, in an undeveloped state.

in partibus (īnfidēlium)

~ in the regions of infidels, i.e. in countries inhabited by unbelievers.

This is used of a bishop holding office in a non-Christian or non-Catholic country and therefore without a see.

1687 in SIR HENRY ELLIS *Original Letters* ser. iii IV.314 The King having . . . recommended Father Phillip Ellis, Dr. Gifford, and Dr. Smith, to be Bishops *in partibus.*

in parvō

~ in miniature, on a small scale.

in pectore

~ in the brest.

This refers to something done or meditated privately and not announced to the general public.

1858 N. WISEMAN *Recollections of the Last Four Popes* vii.333 The Pope made this speech . . . in this form: 'Moreover, *we create* a cardinal of the Holy Roman Church, . . . whom, however, we reserve *in pectore.*

in perpetuum

~ in perpetuity, for ever.

Catullus (ci.10) bids a final farewell at his brother's grave: *atque in perpetuum, frater, ave atque vale* (and for ever, brother, fare thee well). 1642 tr. *Perkins' (John) Profitable booke, treating of the lawes of England* iii.para.239 If Lands or Tenements bee devised by Will, unto a man and his Assignees, *in perpetuum.*

in plēnō

~ in full.

in pontificālibus

~ in pontificals, in the proper vestments of a pope, cardinal, archbishop, etc.

1494 R. FABYAN *Chronicles* vii.607 The deane and the chanons of Paulys, with whom also *in pontificalibus* came the archebysshop of Caunterbury.

in posse
∼ in possibility, in potential existence.

Generally in conjunction with IN ESSE

1592 B. GREENE *Defence of conny catching* in *Works* (Grosart) XI.44 To strippe him of all that his purse had in Esse, or his credyt in Posse.

in potentiā
∼ *same meaning as last entry.*

1601 A. COPLEY *Answere to a Letter of a Jesuited Gent.* 26 No compleate head in *esse* but only in *potentia*.

1612 B. JONSON *Alchemist* II.iii. sig. E1 The Egg is ... a Chicken, in Potentia.

in praesentī
∼ at the present time.

in prīncipiō
∼ in the beginning.

These opening words of St John's gospel, which were regarded with special reverence and even held to have magical power, were recited so engagingly by Chaucer's Friar (General Prologue to the *Canterbury Tales* 254) that, as the poet tells us with a smiling pretence of approval, he could charm the widow of her mite:

For thogh a widwe hadde noght a sho,
So plesaunt was his '*In principio*,'
Yet wolde he have a ferthing, er he wente.

in propriā persōnā
∼ in one's own person.

1654 GAYTON *Pleasant notes upon Don Quixot* Notes III.vii.113 He Knight-Errant, if he steale *in propria persona*, is Uncalendred for ever.

in pūrīs nātūrālibus
∼ in one's natural state, stark naked.

inquiētum est cor nostrum, dōnec requiēscat in tē
∼ our heart is unsettled until it finds rest in you (i.e. in God).

AUGUSTINE *Confessions* I.i.1.

in rē
∼ in the matter of, referring to.

1877 *Times* 18 Jan. 11/4 Court of Bankruptcy . . . In re B. and L. Harris. This
was an adjourned sitting for public examination. The bankrupts, Messrs.
Benjamin and Lawrence Harris, were merchants.

in rērum nātūrā
∼ in the nature of things, i.e. in nature, in the physical world.

in saecula saeculōrum
∼ literally, 'for ages of ages', i.e. to all eternity, for ever.

īnsalūtātō hospite
∼ without saying goodbye to one's host, i.e. 'making a quick
getaway'.

īnsānus omnis furere crēdit cēterōs
∼ all madmen think that everyone else is mad.

The saying suggests that we are blind to our own faults and even impute
them to our fellow men and women.

in scirpō nōdum quaeris
∼ literally, 'you're looking for a knot in a bulrush', i.e. you are
giving yourself pointless trouble.

PLAUTUS *Menaechmi* 247.

īnsculpsit
∼ he/she engraved it.

This word, in conjunction with the engraver's name, used to be placed at
the bottom of an engraving to acknowledge his work.

in sē
∼ in itself.

1868 W. JAMES *Letter*. 5 Apr. in R. B. PERRY *The thought and character of William
James* (1935) I.xv.269 To the Greeks a thing was evil only transiently and
accidentally . . . Bystanders could remain careless and untouched—no
after-brooding, no disinterested hatred of it *in se*, and questioning of its
right to darken the world.

in sitū
∼ in its (original) place; in position.

1740 W. STUKELEY *Stonehenge* iv.21 Eleven of them are standing *in situ*.

īnstar omnium
∼ worth the whole lot of them.

CICERO *Brutus* li.191. Cicero is referring to the Athenian philosopher Plato.

in statū nāscendī

∼ in the process of creation, formation, or construction.

1890 W. JAMES *The principles of psychology* II.xvii.11 Black can only be felt in contrast to white . . . and in like manner a smell, a taste, a touch, only, so to speak, *in statu nascendi*, whilst, when the stimulus continues, all sensation disappears.

in statū pūpillārī

∼ as a pupil or ward; under scholastic discipline; at the universities, referring to all who have not attained the degree of Master.

1855 *Newspaper and general reader's pocket companion* 571 A young Englishman . . . while still in statu pupillari.

in statū quō (ante, prius, or nunc)

∼ in the same state (as formerly (*ante* and *prius*) or now (*nunc*)).

1602 W. WATSON *Decacordon* 174 The seculars are but *in statu quo prius*, and cannot be in a worse then they are in at this present.

integer vītae

∼ blameless in one's life.

HORACE *Odes* I.xxii.1. The poet claims that the blameless have nothing to fear amid the dangers to which humans are exposed. At any rate, a monstrous wolf did not attack *him* when he was wandering in the woods composing a poem about his girlfriend.

intelligentī pauca

∼ literally, 'a few things for the man who understands', i.e. a word to the wise.

A wise man does not need a long lesson.

inter alia

∼ among other things or matters.

1665 SIR T. HERBERT *A relation of some years travaile* (1677) 195 Three errant Monks . . . make strange discoveries as well as descriptions of places; and *inter alia* of Cambalu.

inter aliōs

∼ among other people.

1670 J. HACKET *Scrinia reserata, a memorial offer'd to the great deservings of John Williams* ii. (1693) 152 The Lords produce *inter alios*, John Duke of Lancaster.

inter caesa et porrēcta

∼ literally, 'between the slaughter (of the sacrificial victim) and its being laid (on the altar)', i.e. there's many a slip 'twixt cup and lip.

CICERO *Ad Atticum* v.18. Aulus Gellius (*Noctes Atticae* XIII.xviii) attributes to Cato the Elder a parallel saying: 'I have often heard that many things can come between mouth and morsel.'

inter canem et lupum

∼ literally, 'between dog and wolf', i.e. between the devil and the deep blue sea.

This proverbial expression is echoed by Plautus in *Casina* 971 when a randy old man finds himself threatened by a menacing slave and an intimidating wife. Horace exploits it at *Satires* II.ii.64 where the choice must be made between the two extremes of gluttony and meanness.

interim fit aliquid

∼ something happens in the meantime.

Based on TERENCE *Andria* 314. A character in Terence's play expresses the hope that 'something will turn up' to prevent an event he dreads (i.e. the marriage to somebody else of a girl he wants for himself).

inter nōs

∼ between ourselves, confidentially.

Cf. French *entre nous*.

1714 J. SWIFT *Horace, Satires* ii.6. Where all that passes *inter nos* Might be proclaimed at Charing-cross.

inter parēs (plural interrēs)

∼ between equals.

See also PRIMUS INTER PARES.

inter pōcula

∼ literally, 'among the drinking cups', i.e. over drinks, in our cups.

interrēx (plural interrēgēs)

∼ one who holds the supreme authority in a state during an interregnum.

1579/80 T. NORTH *Plutarch* (1612) 308 The regents at that time called *interreges*.

in terrōrem

~ as a warning, in order to terrify or deter others.

1612 J. CHAMBERLAIN in *Court & Times of James I* (1848) I.213 Most men believe ... that only it was done *in terrōrem*.

inter sē

~ between or among themselves.

1845 R. FORD *A hand-book for travellers in Spain* i.223 The 'little wars' which Spaniards wage *inter se*.

inter spem et metum

~ between hope and fear.

inter vīvōs

~ between living persons, especially of a gift as opposed to a legacy.

1837 T. LEWIN *Pract. Treat. Law Trusts & Trustees* vi.86 The Bank of England cannot be made a trustee, for the Company will not enter notice of instruments *inter vivos* upon their books.

in totidem verbīs

~ in so many words

in tōtō

~ as a whole, completely, without exception.

First recorded use in English 1639.

1811 G. CONSTABLE *Letter* 31 Dec. in J. Constable *Correspondence* (1962) 1.73 If my opinion was requested it would not be to give up your female acquaintance in toto.

intrā mūrōs

~ within the walls

in trānsitū

~ in passing, on the way.

1620 *Reliquiae Wottonianae* (1654) 334 I had, *in transitu*, conferred with him your Christian ends.

intrā vīrēs

~ literally, 'within the powers', i.e. within the powers or legal authority of a corporation or person. Cf. ULTRA VIRES.

in ūsū

~ in use.

in ūsum Delphīnī

∼ literally, 'for the use of the Dauphin', i.e. expurgated.

The Delphin Classics, a set of Latin classics edited in France by thirty-nine scholars for the use of the son of Louis XIV, were purged of all potentially corrupting matter. The heir to the French throne was called the Dauphin after the dolphin (*delphinus* in Latin, *dauphin* in French) on his coat of arms.

in uterō

∼ in the uterus or womb, unborn.

1713 W. CHESELDEN, *Anatomy of Humane Body* IV.iii.170 It seems highly necessary, that the Ducts thro' which the Body receives Nourishment after the Birth, shou'd be kept open by a Fluid passing that way whilst it is *in Utero*.

in utrumque parātus

∼ ready for both of two possibilities, i.e. ready to face either triumph or death with equal sang-froid.

VIRGIL *Aeneid* ii.61. In Virgil's poem the Greek Sinon has the task of tricking the Trojans into taking the wooden horse into Troy. Either his cunning will succeed—as proves to be the case—or he will be unmasked and killed.

in vacuō

∼ in a vacuum or empty space.

1660 J. EVELYN *Diary* (1872) I.364 Various experiments *in vacuo*.

in vīnō veritās

∼ (there is) truth in wine, i.e. truth comes out under the influence of alcohol; a drunken person tells the truth.

The Greek on which this is based is ἐν οἴνῳ ἀλήθεια, attributed to Alcaeus (7th century BC).

1545 R. TAVERNER tr. Erasmus' *Adages* (edn. 2) H5v In wyne is trouthe.

1934 R. GRAVES *Claudius the God* ix The man who made the proverb 'There's truth in wine' must have been pretty well soaked when he wrote it.

invītā Minervā

∼ literally, 'when Minerva (Roman goddess of wisdom) is unwilling', i.e. when one is not in the vein or mood, without inspiration. The expression is found in Horace's *Ars Poetica* (385) where he writes, 'You [the poet] will say nothing and do nothing when Minerva is unwilling.'

1584 R. SCOT *Discoverie of Witchcraft* XII.iii.219 It should be unto them (*invita Minerva*) to banket or danse with Minerva.

in vitrō

~ literally 'in glass', i.e. in a test tube, culture dish, etc; hence, outside a living body, under artificial conditions.

The present currency of the phrase is due to the practice of *in vitro* fertilization.

1894 G. M. GOULD *A dictionary of new medical terms* 623/2 *In vitro*, in the glass; applied to phenomena that are observed in experiments carried out in the laboratory with microörganisms, digestive ferments, and other agents, but that may not necessarily occur within the living body.

in vīvō

~ within the living organism.

The opposite of IN VITRO.

1901 *Journal of Experimental Medicine* V.355 Serum obtained by immunising with one race did not necessarily give more than a trace of reaction in vitro and none whatever in vivo when tested with another race.

iocī causā

~ for the sake of a joke.

ipsa quidem pretium virtūs sibi

~ literally, 'virtue itself pays the price to itself', i.e. virtue is its own reward.

CLAUDIAN *De Consulatu Fl. Mallii Theodori* 1. Derived from OVID *Ex Ponto* II.iii.12, where the poet observes that you couldn't find one man in a thousand who really believes this.

Cf. 1509 A. BARCLAY *The Shyp of Folys* 10v Vertue hath no rewarde.

ipse dīxit

~ he himself said.

This is used of a mere assertion, a dogmatic statement or dictum, totally unsupported save by the speaker's authority. It is the Latin for the Greek words (αὐτὸς ἔφα) used of Pythagoras by his followers and is quoted by Cicero (*De Natura Deorum* I.v.10).

ipsissima verba

~ the very words, i.e. the precise words used by a writer or speaker.

1807 R. SOUTHEY *Letters from England* (1856) II.40 Last night I was in too much haste to look for the *ipsissima verba* of Fuller.

ipsō factō
~ by that very fact, by the fact itself.

First recorded use in English 1548.

1647 Bp. ROBERT SANDERSON *A Sermon* II.214 By taking Christendom upon us at our Baptism, we did *ipso facto* renounce the world.

ipsō iūre
~ by operation of the law itself.

First recorded use in English 1909.

1913 *Act 3 & 4 Geo. V* c. 20 para. 97 The act and warrant of confirmation in favour of the trustee shall ipso iure transfer to and vest in him ... the whole property of the debtor.

īra furor brevis est
~ anger is a short-lived madness.

HORACE *Epistles* I.ii.62. The poet urges us to keep control of emotions lest they gain control of us.

īte, missa est
~ Go, the Mass is finished.

The final words of the Roman Catholic Mass in the Latin service.

iūbilāte Deō
~ rejoice in God.

These words open Psalm 100, used as a canticle in the Anglican service. It is frequently abbreviated to JUBILATE.

iūcundī āctī labōrēs
~ completed labours are pleasant.

CICERO *De Finibus* II.cv.7. Cicero here gives a Latin translation of a line from Euripides, *Andromeda* (fragment 133 Nauck): 'But it is pleasant to look back on toils once one has come through them safely.' Cf. FORSAN ET HAEC MEMINISSE IUVABIT.

iūdex damnātur ubi nocēns absolvitur
~ the judge is condemned when the guilty is acquitted.

PUBLILIUS SYRUS *Sententiae* I.28.

iūniōrēs ad labōrēs
~ the younger (people should go) to work.

Iuppiter hostis
~ Jupiter (my) enemy.

VIRGIL *Aeneid* xii.895. The Italian prince Turnus, about to die at the hands of the Trojan Aeneas, here expresses his awareness that the king of the gods is against him.

Iuppiter pluvius
~ Jupiter, the rain-giver.

TIBULLUS I.vii.26. One of the functions of Jupiter, king of the gods, was to control the weather.

Iuppiter tonāns
~ Jupiter, the thunderer.

Jupiter, king of the gods, wielded a thunderbolt, of which the guilty should beware.

iūre dīvīnō
~ by divine law.

iūre hūmānō
~ by human law.

iūs cīvīle
~ civil law.

iūs et norma loquendī
~ the right and rule of speech.

HORACE *Ars Poetica* 172. Horace makes the point that some expressions fall out of currency while others have a second birth. It is all a matter of usage, the arbitrator and 'the right and rule of speech'.

iūs gentium
~ the law of nations.

1548 Bp. JOHN *A declaration of the ten holy commandements* HOOPER *Commmandm.* iii.31 They shuld observe the commune lawes usyd among all people whiche is callid ius gentium.

iūs prīmae noctis
~ right of the first night.

It has been believed that by this custom, known in French as *droit de seigneur*, the feudal lord had the right to sleep with every bride on his estate on her wedding night.

1887 F. K. WISCHNEWETZKY tr. Engels's *Condition of Working-Class in England in 1844* 99 Factory servitude . . . confers the *jus primae noctis* upon the master . . . If the master is mean enough, . . . his mill is also his harem.

iūs suum cuique

∼ to each man his rights, to each man his due.

JUSTINIAN *Digesta Iustiniani* I.i.10.1 (quoting Ulpian).

iūstitia omnibus

∼ justice for all.

This is the motto of the district of Columbia in New York City.

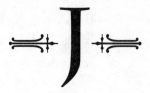

There was no letter 'j' in Latin, but in English the consonantal 'i' in Latin words (as for example in *ius*) has often been written as 'j'. Where 'j' is the first letter of a word or phrase, look it up under 'i'.

Kȳrie eleison
~ Lord, have mercy.

The Latinized version of the Greek words occurring in the Greek text of the gospel according to St Matthew (xv.22 & xvii.15) and elsewhere in the Bible. These are the words of a short petition used in various offices of the Eastern and Roman Churches, especially at the beginning of the Mass. Musical settings of the words are frequent, especially as the first movement of a Mass.

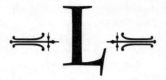

LSD

∼ pounds, shillings and pence, in the former English coinage.

L = *lībra* (a pound); s = *solidus* (a shilling); d = *dēnārius* (a penny). There is a humorous expression *L.S.Deism*, meaning 'worship of money'.

1853 HOOD *Dead Robbery* i But perhaps, of all the felonies de se, . . . Two-thirds have been through want of *L.s.d.*!

labōrāre est ōrāre

∼ to work is to pray.

The motto of the Benedictine order of monks.

labor omnia vincit

∼ labour conquers all things.

An adaptation of a statement of Virgil's in the *Georgics* (i.145).

labōrum dulce lēnīmen

∼ the sweet solace of our labours.

Horace here (*Odes* I.xxxii.14–15) refers to his lyre, i.e. to his poetry, which proves so great a pleasure to him.

lābuntur et imputantur

∼ (the moments) slip away and are laid to our account.

An inscription on sundials.

lachryma Christī

∼ literally, 'Christ's tear (or tears)', used of a strong and sweet red wine of southern Italy.

1611 T. CORYAT *Crudities* (1776) II.72 Their *Lagryme di Christo* . . . so toothsome and delectable to the taste.

lacrimae rērum

∼ literally, 'the tears of things', i.e. the tragedy inherent in human existence.

These famous words from Virgil (*Aeneid* i.462) are often taken as a Virgilian statement of his view of life as a vale of tears. In fact, in context they simply mean that people are sympathetic in that they cry over the sufferings of others. The Trojan Aeneas has found on the walls of the temple of Juno in distant Carthage a series of pictures of the Trojan War, which he has lived through, and takes it that the subject matter of these betokens sympathy with the sufferings of his people in that war.

lāpsus calamī
~ a slip of the pen.

1893 *Nation* (N.Y.) 2 Mar. 165/2 The following . . . is a lapsus calami whose occurrence it is quite impossible to understand.

lāpsus linguae
~ a slip of the tongue.

1667 J. DRYDEN *Martin Mar-all* iii. (1668) 28 What have I done besides a little lapsus linguae?

lāpsus memoriae
~ a slip of the memory.

larēs et penātēs
~ household gods, the home.

First recorded use (of *lares*) in English 1586. In the hall (*atrium*) of a Roman house the images of these gods would be kept in a cupboard-like shrine, and a small service was likely to be held in their honour every day, presided over by the father of the household. The *lares* were the deified spirits of dead ancestors while the *penates* were the spirits that watched over the larder. The Latin word *et* means 'and'.

Cf. 1600 P. HOLLAND *Livy* viii.ix.287 O yee Lares and domesticall gods.

latet anguis in herbā
~ a snake lurks in the grass.

VIRGIL *Eclogues* iii.93. A Virgilian herdsman warns children gathering flowers of a hidden danger.

laudātor temporis āctī
~ a glorifier of the times gone by.

HORACE *Ars Poetica* 173. The successful poet must target the various age groups in his audience. The old man glories in the days gone by when he was a boy: 'The years as they come bring a lot of advantages with them, but as they go they take a lot away too' (175–6).

laus Deō
  ~ praise be to God.

laus propria sordet
  ~ self-praise is no recommendation.

laus tibi
  ~ literally, 'praise to thee', a name for the white narcissus, *narcissus poeticus*.

1548 W. TURNER *Names of Herbes* (1881) 55 Narcissus . . . wyth a white floure . . . it is called of diverse, whyte Laus tibi, it maye be called also whyte daffadyl.

lēctor benevole
  ~ kind reader.

leve fit, quod bene fertur, onus
  ~ a burden that is cheerfully borne becomes light.

OVID *Amores* I.ii.10. Since this is true, urges the poet, let's give in to love!

lēx domiciliī
  ~ the law of the country in which a person is domiciled; the determination of the rights of a person by establising where, in law, he is domiciled.

1832 BARNEWALL & CRESSWELL *Rep. Cases King's Bench* X.909 The lex domicilii is to be regarded, yet it is not adverted to where the domicile was when the contract was entered into.

lēx forī
  ~ literally, 'the law of the forum' (the city centre where the law courts were), used of the law of the country in which an action is brought, as determining the nature and modes of the proceedings.

1836 H. WHEATON *Elem. Internat. Law* I.ii.ii.188 The extrinsic evidence by which the existence and terms of the contract are to be proved in a foreign tribunal is regulated by the *lex fori*.

lēx locī
  ~ the law of the place, i.e. the law of the country in which a legal transaction is performed, a tort is committed, or a property is situated; frequently followed by a defining word or phrase.

1832 BARNEWALL & CRESSWELL *Rep. Cases King's Bench* X.985 The decisions of both English and Scotch courts shew that the construction of personal contracts depends on the lex loci contractus.

lēx nōn scrīpta

~ the unwritten law, i.e. the common law, derived in English law from precedent, as opposed to the statute or written law.

The provisions of common law have in fact been compiled and printed, but they are not statutes but simply reminders.

lēx tāliōnis

~ the law of retaliation; 'an eye for an eye, a tooth for a tooth'.

Cf. Exodus xxi.23–5. First recorded use in English 1597.

1821 JEFFERSON *Autobiographical Writings* (1892) 1.68 For other felonies should be substituted hard labor ... and in some cases the *Lex Talionis*.

licet

~ it is allowed.

The word signifies granting of permission. Its opposite is *non licet* (it is not allowed).

līterae hūmāniōrēs

~ the more humane studies, i.e. the humanities, secular learning as opposed to divinity. At the University of Oxford it refers to the study of Greek and Roman classical literature, philosophy, and ancient history.

In classical Latin, the preferred spelling of the first of these two words in *literae*. First recorded use in English 1747.

1760 L. STERNE *Tristram Shandy* (edn. 3) II.xii.61 I would not depreciate what the study of the *Literae humaniores*, at the university, have done for me.

līterātī

~ 'lettered men', i.e. men of letters, the learned class as a whole.

1621 R. BURTON *Anatomy of Melancholy* To Reader (1624) 52 To be ... examined & approued as the literati in China.

littera scrīpta manet

~ the written word remains.

The saying continues, 'The weak word perishes.'

locō citātō (abbreviated to loc. cit.)

~ in the place cited, i.e. in the book, etc., that has previously been quoted.

1854 H. H. MILMAN *History of Latin Christianity* I.ii.iii.149 In the words of the ecclesiastical historian, . . . by such a deed a deep stain was fixed on Cyril and the Church of Alexandria. [fn.] Socrat. loc. cit.

locum tenēns
∼ holding the place (of another); (as noun phrase) a substitute.

In Great Britain now chiefly abbreviated to 'locum' and applied to the deputy of a medical practitioner or of a clergyman. First recorded use in English 1641.

1838 E. LYTTON *Alice* III.ii The old driveller will be my *locum tenens*, till years and renown enable me to become his successor.

locus classicus
∼ a classic passage, i.e. a standard passage, especially one in an ancient author, which is viewed as the principal authority on a subject.

1853 W. BAGEHOT *Collected Works* (1965) I.202 These lines are, as it were, the *locus classicus* of fairy literature.

locus commūnis (plural locī commūnēs)
∼ a commonplace.

1531 T. ELYOT *Governour* i.xiv Hauyng almoste all the places wherof they shal fetche their raisons, called of Oratours *loci communes*, which I omitte to name.

locus dēlictī
∼ the scene of the crime.

locus dēspērātus
∼ a hopeless passage, i.e. a passage in a text transmitted by manuscript whose meaning is so corrupt as to be almost beyond conjecture.

1922 F. KLAEBER (ed.) *Beowulf* 214 This passage remains a 'locus desperatus'.

1970 *Anglia* LXXXVIII.367 Faced with such a *locus desperatus*, even a conscientious editor might decline to grapple afresh with the battered folio.

locus in quō
∼ the place in which (something takes place), the locality of an event, etc.; in law it is used to designate the land on which trespass has been committed.

1717 W. SALKELD *Reports of cases adjudg'd in the court of King's bench* I.94 The Plaintiff demurred, because here are two Places alledged and the Avowant has only answered to the *locus in quo*, &c. which is but one of the two Places.

locus poenitentiae

∼ a place (i.e. opportunity) for repentance; in law it is used of an opportunity allowed to a person to recede from some engagement, so long as some particular step has not been taken. The phrase is taken from the Epistle to the Hebrews xii.17 where St Paul says that Esau 'found no place for repentance, though he sought it carefully with tears'.

1768 J. ERSKINE *An institute of the law of Scotland* iii.ii (1773) 427 The right competent to a party to resile from a bargain concerning land, before he has bound himself by writing is called in our law *locus poenitentiae*.

locus sigillī (abbreviated to LS)

∼ the place of the seal, i.e. the place on a document where the seal is to be placed.

locus standī

∼ literally, 'place of standing', i.e. recognized position; in law, a right to appear in court.

1835 J. W. CROKER *Essays on the early period of the French Revolution* vi (1857) 342 By this daring step Robespierre acquired a kind of *locus standi*.

longō intervāllō

∼ after a long gap.

A shortened form of *proximus, sed longo intervallo* (next (certainly), but at what a vast distance!), based on a phrase in Virgil's description of a foot race (*Aeneid* v. 320).

longum iter est per precepta, breve et efficāx per exempla

∼ long is the way through precepts, short and effective through examples.

SENECA *Letters* vi.5. The usual English form of this saying is 'example is better than precept'.

Cf. *c.* 1400 J. MIRK *Festial* (EETS) 216 Then saythe Seynt Austeyn that an ensampull yn doyng ys more commendabull then ys techyng other [i.e. or] prechyng.

loquitur (abbreviated to loq.)

∼ he/she speaks (a stage direction).

Also used following the speaker's name, as a note to the reader.

1855 W. BAGEHOT in *National Review* Oct. 274 'Remember my joke against you' (Sydney Smith *loquitur*) 'about the moon.'

lucrī bonus est odor ex rē quālibet

~ the smell of money is good wherever it comes from.

JUVENAL xiv.204. In Rome, foul-smelling businesses, such as tanning, were banished to the west bank of the Tiber, away from the main city area. Suetonius (*Vespasian* xxiii) tells the story of how Titus criticized his father, the emperor Vespasian, for putting a tax on public lavatories. Vespasian held a coin from the first payment up to his son's nose and asked him whether it smelt bad. To his son's negative response, Vespasian replied, 'And yet it comes from urine.'

lūcus ā nōn lūcendō

~ the grove (*lucus* in Latin) (is so named) from its *not* shining (*lucendo* in Latin), i.e. a paradoxical or absurd derivation, something of which the essence or qualities are the opposite of what its name suggests.

1711 J. ADDISON *Spectator* 8 May He composd an . . . Epic Poem . . . consisting of four and twenty Books, having entirely banished the Letter *A* from his first Book, which was called *Alpha* (as *Lucus a non lucendo*) because there was not an *Alpha* in it.

1823 BYRON *Don Juan* VI.Iv.248 Thus . . . has been shown 'Lucus a *non* Lucendo', *not* what *was*, But what *was not*; a sort of style that's grown Extremely common in this age.'

lūmen nātūrāle

~ 'natural light', i.e. inborn wisdom.

lūmen siccum

~ dry light, i.e. the dry light of rational knowledge or thought.

1605 F. BACON *Advancement of Learning* ii.f.48 But this same *Lumen siccum*, doth parch and offend most mens watry and soft natures.

1886 MRS CHAPMAN *The Nineteenth Century* If psychological considerations have any meaning, it will be always impossible for women to view the subject [of women's suffrage] *in lumine sicco*.

lupum auribus tenēre

~ literally, 'to hold a wolf by the ears', i.e. to be unable to hold on and afraid to let go, and thus to be in a situation of doubt and difficulty.

TERENCE *Phormio* III.ii.21.

lupus est homō hominī

~ man is wolf to man, i.e. men prey on one another.

PLAUTUS *Asinaria* 495. In a famous speech in Shakespeare's *Troilus and Cressida* (I.iii.75ff.), Ulysses uses the wolf as a climactic image of the mutually destructive chaos which follows the breakdown of hierarchical degree:

Then everything includes itself in power,
Power into will, will into appetite;
And appetite, an universal wolf,
So doubly seconded with will and power,
Must make perforce an universal prey,
And last eat up himself.

lupus in fābulā

~ the wolf in the story (a proverb used of the appearance of a person when he is spoken of), i.e. 'talk of the devil, and he appears.'

TERENCE *Adelphi* IV.i.21.

lupus pilum mūtat, nōn mentem

~ the wolf changes his coat, not his character.

Cf. the English proverb, 'The leopard does not change his spots.'

lūsus nātūrae

~ a freak (literally, 'a sportive action') of nature, i.e. a production of nature deviating markedly from the normal type, or having the appearance of being the result of a sportive design.

1661 T. FULLER *Worthies, Gloucestershire* (1662) I.351 Others more probably account them [fossils] to be *Lusus Naturae*.

lūx mundī

~ the light of the world.

These words from the Vulgate (John viii.12) are Jesus' description of himself: 'I am the light of the world: he that followeth me shall not walk in darkness, but shall have the light of life.' Today they are often used to refer to Holman Hunt's famous painting of Christ at a door holding a lamp (1854) which hangs in Keble College, Oxford. An allegory of Christ knocking at the door of the human soul, it brought Hunt his first success.

macte virtūte

~ go on in your valour/virtue.

Used by Cicero, Virgil, and Livy. This is the Latin equivalent of English 'good luck!', 'bravo!', 'well done!' Rather surprisingly, the grim Roman censor Cato the Elder used these encouraging words to an aristocratic young man he saw coming out of a brothel (HORACE *Satires* I.ii.31–2). His point was that it was better to go there than to commit adultery.

magister artis ingeniīque largītor venter

~ the belly is the teacher of art and the dispenser of genius, i.e. necessity is the mother of invention.

PERSIUS *Satires* Prologue 10. The satirist self-deprecatingly explains why he is writing his verse. The prospect of cash renders all sorts of untalented people poetical.

Magister Artium (abbreviated to MA)

~ Master of Arts, the intermediate degree at universities.

Magna C(h)arta

~ the Great Charter of English personal and political liberty, obtained from King John in 1215, repeatedly confirmed, and appealed to in all disputes between the sovereign and his subjects, till the establishment of constitutional government.

1568 R. GRAFTON *Chronicles* II.118 This Parliament king Edwards lawes were again restored, & Magna carta confirmed.

magna cīvitās, magna sōlitūdō

~ a great city (is) a great solitude, i.e. one feels very lonely in the city.

magnā cum laude

~ with great distinction.

Designating a degree, diploma, etc., of a higher standard than the average (though not the highest—then *summa* replaces *magna*).

1900 *Dialect Notes* II.13 A few words or phrases of direct Latin importation used at some of the older institutions ... more commonly *cum laude*, *magna* or *summa cum laude* for the degree of honor attained in studies.

magnae spēs altera Rōmae
∼ the second hope of great Rome, i.e. the second man of the state, the heir to the throne, etc.

VIRGIL (*Aeneid* xii.168) uses the phrase of Ascanius, the son of his hero Aeneas.

magna est vēritās, et praevalet
∼ truth is great, and it prevails.

Based on 4 Ezra vii.114 in the Vulgate, the Latin version of the Bible.

magna māter
∼ the great mother, a fertility goddess.

1845 *Encylopaedia metropolitana* XVII.481/2 *Cybele*, otherwise known as Ops, Rhea, Vesta, ... Idaea Mater, Magna Mater, Mater Deorum, Bona Dea, and Tellus.

magnās inter opēs inops
∼ poor amid great riches.

magnificat
∼ literally, 'it magnifies'.

The first word in the Vulgate of the hymn of the Virgin Mary in response to the Annunciation. She sings 'My soul doth magnify the Lord' (*Magnificat anima mea Dominum*), and the hymn (Luke i.46–55) is used as a canticle at evensong or vespers. There are many musical settings of this canticle.

magnī nōminis umbra
∼ the (mere) shadow of a great name.

LUCAN i.135. Comparing Pompey and Caesar before the outbreak of the civil war between them (49–46 BC), Lucan creates an expressive image of the former as a grand has-been, reliant on his name. Pompey, who was in fact only six years older than Caesar, had been given the surname 'the Great' by the senate in 81 BC, so that there is a play on words here: the great name is literally the name 'Great'.

magnum bonum
~ a great good.

This is also used of a particular kind of large yellow cooking-plum, a kind of potato, and a large-barrelled steel pen.

magnum opus
~ the 'chief work' of an author.

1704 J. SWIFT *Tale of Tub* v.116 His Account of the *Opus magnum* is extreemly poor and deficient.

1791 J. BOSWELL *Letter to Rev. W. Temple* (1857) 406 My *magnum opus*, the 'Life of Dr. Johnson' . . . is to be published on Monday, 16th May.

maior ē longinquō reverentia
~ greater respect from a distance, i.e. familiarity breeds contempt.

Cf. *c.* 1386 CHAUCER *Tale of Melibee* 1. 1685 Men seyn that 'over-greet hoomlynesse engendreth dispreisynge'.

malā fidē
~ in bad faith.

Used of actions and titles which are fraudulent or sham.

mala parta, male dīlābuntur
~ things ill-gotten slip away in evil ways, i.e. ill-gotten goods are never profitable.

CICERO *Philippic* II.xxvii.65. Cicero quotes Naevius in denouncing Mark Antony's seizure of the estate of Pompey the Great.

Cf. 1519 W. HORMAN *Vulgaria* 77 Euyll gotten ryches wyll neuer proue longe.

malesuāda Famēs
~ Hunger that urges people to crime.

VIRGIL *Aeneid* vi.257. Hunger is one of the grim or gloomy personifications which crowd at the entry to Virgil's hell.

malīs avibus
~ literally, 'with bad (i.e. unfavourable) birds', i.e. under bad auspices.

The Romans frequently based their predictions on the flight of birds.

malum in sē (plural mala in sē)
~ literally, 'something evil in itself, i.e. something intrinsically evil or wicked.

1623 J. WILLIAMS *Letter* 30 Aug. in J. Hacket *Scrinia Reserata* (1693) i.157 But to grant a Pardon even for a thing that is *malum in se*.

manus manum lavat
~ literally, 'hand washes hand', i.e. I'll scratch your back if you'll scratch mine.

SENECA *Apocolocyntosis* ix.6. The satirist quotes a proverb which insists on mutual help.

mare clausum
~ literally, 'a closed sea', i.e. a sea under the jurisdiction of a particular country.

This term (and MARE LIBERUM) originated during the struggle between England and the Netherlands in the seventeenth century.

1652 M. NEDHAM tr. Selden's *Of Dominion of Sea* sig. g1 Mare Clausum is the Sea possessed in a private manner, or so secluded both by Right and Occupation, that it ceaseth to be common.

mare līberum
~ literally, 'a free sea', i.e. a sea open to all nations.

1652 M. NEDHAM tr. Selden's *Of Dominion of Sea* sig. a2 This People [the Netherlanders] ... carried out their design ... by ... a daily intrusion upon the Territorie by Sea, that in time they durst plead and print *Mare Liberum* ... to defie the Dominion of England over the Sea.

Cf. MARE CLAUSUM.

margarītās ante porcōs
~ pearls before swine.

MATTHEW vii.6: 'Give not that which is holy unto the dogs, neither cast ye your pearls before swine.'

Māter Dolōrōsa
~ literally, 'sorrowful mother', a title of the Virgin Mary, emphasizing her role in the Passion of Christ; a representation, in painting or sculpture, of the Virgin Mary sorrowing; also, a woman who has the attributes of the sorrowful mother.

The term probably originated in the medieval Latin hymn beginning *Stabat mater dolorosa Iuxta crucem lacrimosa* (the sorrowful mother was standing near the cross in tears).

1800 J. DALLAWAY *Anecdotes of Arts in England* 516 He has a mater dolorosa and a boy playing on a lute by Guido.

1872 G. ELIOT *Middlemarch* IV.viii.lxxx.283 Dorothea's face ... had the pale cheeks and pink eyelids of a *mater dolorosa*.

māterfamiliās (plural mātrēs familiārum)
∼ the mother of a household.

First recorded use in English 1756.

1861 *Wheat & Tares* ii.13 Mrs. Leslie seemed rather overpowered by her responsibilities as Materfamilias. Cf. PATERFAMILIAS.

mātre pulchrā fīliā pulchrior
∼ daughter more beautiful than your beautiful mother.

HORACE *Odes* I.xvi.1. Horace asks the daughter, with whom he is in love, to destroy some scurrilous lyrics he sent to her, or perhaps to the mother, during a previous love affair.

maxima dēbētur puerō reverentia
∼ the greatest reverence is due to the boy, i.e. to the innocence of youth.

JUVENAL xiv.47. Juvenal advises his addressee Fuscinus to think twice about corrupting the young.

maximus in minimīs
∼ very great in very little things.

mea culpa
∼ through my own fault, a phrase from the prayer of confession in the Latin liturgy of the Church; used more generally as an exclamation of repentance, and as the name of such an exclamation; also *mea maxima culpa* (through my very great fault).

1374 CHAUCER *Troïlus & Criseyde* ii.525 Now, *mea culpa*, lord, I me repente!

1958 *Times* 17 Oct. 17/1 Eisenstein made a public *mea culpa* at the time in the form of an open letter to the Committee.

mediocria firma
∼ the middle condition in life is the safe one.

mediō dē fonte lepōrum surgit amārī aliquid quod in ipsīs flōribus angat
∼ from the middle of the spring of joys there rises something bitter to give us grief even amid the flowers.

LUCRETIUS *De Rerum Natura* iv.1133–4. The realization that one is happy can lead perversely to disturbed thoughts which eclipse the happiness.

mediō tūtissimus ībis
∼ you will travel most safely in the middle.

OVID *Metamorphoses* ii.137. Ovid puts these words into the mouth of the sun god, Apollo, who is advising his son Phaethon how to drive the chariot of the sun, which he is reluctantly allowing him to do—with disastrous results.

medium tenuēre beātī
~ the happy have held the middle course.

membrum virīle
~ the virile member, the penis.

1732 P. SKIPPON *Journal* in J. Churchil *Collection of voyages and travels* VI (1732) A Frenchman, that seeing the postboy fall down dead with the extremity of cold, opened his codpiece, and rub'd his *Membrum virile* with snow, till he recovered him.

1991 J. BANES *Talking it Over* v.64 There we stood, two rivals as yet quite unaware they were rivals, each grasping his *membrum virile*—should I offer the groom some tips as to its deployment?

mementō morī
~ literally, 'remember that you must die', used of a warning of death, and of a reminder of death, such as a skull or other symbolical object.

First recorded use in English 1592.

1596 SHAKESPEARE *1 Henry IV* III.iii.34 I make as good use of it, as many a man doth of a Deaths-Head, or a *Memento Mori*.

memorābilia
~ memorable or noteworthy things.

1806–7 J. BERESFORD *The miseries of human life* (1826) ii.Introduction Let us at once produce our memorabilia and proceed to exchange their contents.

memoriā in aeternā
~ in everlasting remembrance.

memoriter
~ from memory, by heart.

1612 J. BRINSLEY *Ludus literarius or the grammar schoole* xiii. (1627) 178 All the Theames of this Author being then written of and pronounced by them memoriter.

mendācem memorem esse oportet
~ a liar ought to have a good memory.

QUINTILIAN *Institutio Oratoria* IV.ii.

Cf. 1542 T. WYATT *Poetical Works* (1858) p. xxxvii They say, 'He that will lie well must have a good remembrance, that he agree in all points with himself, lest he be spied.'

Cf. 1990 *Washington Times* 7 Mar. F1 They say a liar has to have a good memory. In that case, Mr. Reagan's testimony is proof of his honesty.

mēns agitat mōlem
~ a mind sets the mass in motion, i.e. mind animates matter.

VIRGIL *Aeneid* vi.727. The ghost of Anchises explains to his son Aeneas the nature of the universe. Cf. Pope, *Essay on Man* (i.267–8):

All are but parts of one stupendous whole,
Whose body Nature is, and God the soul.

and Wordsworth, *Tintern Abbey*:

A motion and a spirit, that impels
All thinking things, all objects of all thought,
And rolls through all things.

mēns rea
~ literally, 'guilty mind', i.e. the criminal state of mind accompanying an act which condemns the perpetrator of the act to criminal punishment; criminal intent.

1861 LEIGH & CAVE *Crown Cases Reserved* (1866) 53 The *mens rea* is an essential ingredient in every offence.

mēns sāna in corpore sānō
~ a healthy mind in a healthy body.

JUVENAL x.356. The poet suggests that this combination is one worth praying for.

mēns sibi cōnscia rēctī
~ a mind conscious within itself of right, i.e. one's own inner knowledge that one has done right.

VIRGIL *Aeneid* i.604. Aeneas here speaks of himself.

merum sal
~ pure salt, i.e. true good sense or wit.

LUCRETIUS iv.1162. In a famous denunciation of women, the poet notes that the eye of a loving man can view a stunted female as a sparkling wit (*merum sal*) and one of the Graces.

meum [and] tuum
~ 'mine and thine'; what is one's own and what is another's.

A popular phrase to express the rights of property.

1594 R. GREENE & T. LODGE *Looking-gl.* (1598) C iij What, wooe my subiects wife that honoureth me.—Tut, Kings this *meum, tuum* should not know.

mīles glōriōsus (plural mīlitēs glōriōsī)

~ bragging soldier. The name of a comedy by Plautus, used allusively to designate a braggart soldier.

1917 K. M. WESTAWAY *Original Element in Plautus* ii.28 Other plays of Plautus contain *milites gloriosi* of smaller fame.

1950 A. BONJOUR *Digressions in Beowulf* 18 In spite of Beowulf's biting allusion to Grendel's security, we should not take this as an entirely idle vaunt of some *miles gloriosus*.

mīlitat omnis amāns

~ every lover is a soldier.

OVID *Amores* I.ix.1. Ovid sets out on a wonderfully entertaining series of analogies between the life of the lover and that of the soldier.

mīllennium (plural mīllennia)

~ a period of thousand years; also, a thousandth anniversary.

1711 Bp. THOMAS KEN *Hymnarium* in *Poetical Works* (1721) II.54 They on one Theme Milleniums spend.

1840 T. DE QUINCEY *Modern Superstition* in *Works* (1862) III.341 We may pass by a vast transition of two and a half millennia.

mīrābile dictū

~ wonderful to relate.

VIRGIL *Georgics* ii.30.

1831 *Athenaeum* 12 Mar. 172/3 An unassuming young female relative, whom she gives in marriage to the son of her (*mirabile dictu!*) honest attorney.

mīrābile vīsū

~ wonderful to behold.

OVID *Fasti* iii.31.

miserābile vulgus

~ the wretched rabble.

miserēre

~ have mercy.

Psalm 51 (50 in the Vulgate), beginning *Miserere mei Deus* (Have mercy upon me, O God), is one of the Penitential Psalms and has often been set to music.

Missa solemnis
~ literally, 'solemn Mass', i.e. High Mass.

mōbile perpetuum
See PERPETUUM MOBILE.

mōbile vulgus
~ the fickle mob

STATIUS *Silvae* II.ii.123. The word 'mob' is in fact an abbreviation of this term.

modus agendī
~ literally, 'the manner of operation', i.e. the mode in which a thing act or operates.

1849 HENRY M. NOAD *A course of eight lectures; on electricity, galvanism, magnetism, and electro-magnetism* (edn. 3) 29 Scientific men are not agreed as to the *modus agendi* of the amalgam applied to the rubber.

modus operandī
~ a mode of operating: the way in which a thing, cause, etc. operates; (in more recent use) the way in which a person goes to work.

1654 R. WHITLOCK *Zootomia, or observations on the present manners of the English* 222 Because their Causes, or their *modus operandi* (which is but the Application of the Cause to the Effect) doth not fall under Demonstration.

1894 K. GRAHAME *Pagan Papers* 86 It would hardly be in the public interest to disclose his *modus operandi*.

modus vīvendī
~ a mode of living, a working arrangement between contending parties, pending the settlement of matters in debate.

1879 *Notes & Queries* ser.v.XII.109 'Modus Vivendi'—This formula is in daily use to express a practical compromise.

mōlē ruit suā
~ it falls in ruin by its own weight.

HORACE *Odes* III.iv.65. Horace insists on the self-destructive nature of force when it is not tempered by good counsel.

mōns Veneris
~ the more or less prominent fatty eminence covering the pubic area of a woman.

First recorded use in English 1621.

1857 W. R. BULLOCK tr. *Cazeaux Treatise on midwifery* 39 The Mons Veneris is a rounded eminence . . . situated in front of the pubis, and surmounting the vulva.

mōnstrum horrendum, īnfōrme, ingēns
~ a fearful monster, mis-shapen, vast.

VIRGIL *Aeneid* iii.658. Virgil's hero here describes the horrific one-eyed monster, the Cyclops Polyphemus.

monūmentum aere perennius
~ a monument more enduring than bronze.

Horace launches his poem (*Odes* III.xxx) with this insistence on the immortality of his poetry, which, he says, will last as long as the high priest and vestal virgin climb the Capitoline Hill. It has in fact outlasted the priest and the vestal by many centuries.

morātōrium
~ (in law) a legal authorization to a debtor to postpone payment for a certain time; a postponement, an agreed delay, a deliberate temporary suspension (of some activity, etc.).

First recorded use in English 1875.

1972 *Nature* 17 Mar. 94/1 A provision calling for a five-year moratorium on the killing of all ocean mammals.

mōre maiōrum
~ according to the custom of our ancestors.

moritūrī tē salūtant
~ those who are about to die salute you, the salutation of gladiators to the Roman emperor.

SUETONIUS *Claudius* xxi.6.

1704 B. KENNETT *Antiquities of Rome* (edn. 3) II.iii.269 The Naumachiae of Claudius which he presented on the Fucine Lake before he drain'd it, deserve to be particularly mention'd, not more for the greatness of the Show, than for the Behaviour of the Emperour: who when the Combatants pass'd before him with so melancholy a Greeting as, Ave imperator, morituri te salutant, return'd in Answer, Avete vos.

mors certa, hōra incerta
~ death is certain, the hour (of death) uncertain.

mors omnibus commūnis
~ death is common to all.

mortuī nōn mordent

∼ dead men don't bite, i.e. dead men are no longer a danger.

ERASMUS *Adages* III.vi. Erasmus adapts the Greek of PLUTARCH *Pompey* lxxvi.

mōtū propriō

∼ of one's own volition, on one's own initiative, spontaneously.

1603 C. HEYDON *Defence of Judicial Astrology* xxi.447 But the Moone and other Planets moove also motu proprio.

multīs ille bonīs flēbilis occidit

∼ he has died bewailed by many good people.

HORACE *Odes* I.xxiv.9. The poet laments one Quintilius.

multum in parvō

∼ much in little, i.e. a great deal in a small compass; much information communicated in few words.

First recorded use in English 1732.

1825 [S. MAUNDER] (title) The Little Lexicon; or, Multum in Parvo of the English Language.

mundus vult dēcipī, ergō dēcipiātur

∼ the world wants to be deceived, so let it be deceived!

Cf. POPULUS VULT DECIPI, . . .

mūtātīs mūtandīs

∼ 'things being changed that have to be changed', i.e. with the necessary changes; with due alteration of details.

First recorded use in English 1498.

1962 S. E. FINER *Man on Horseback* ii.6 What is said of the army here is to taken also to apply, *mutatis mutandis*, to the air force and the navy.

mūtātō nōmine

∼ 'the name being changed', i.e. applicable in a transferred context if the name of the person, place, etc. is altered accordingly.

HORACE *Satires* I.i.69. Cf. DE TE FABULA NARRATUR.

1621 R. BURTON *Anatomy of Melancholy* (Democritus to the Reader) 37 Accounting it an excellent thing . . . to make our selues merry with other mens obliquities, when as he himselfe is more faultie than the rest, *mutato nomine de te fabula narratur*, he may take himselfe by the nose for a foole.

N

nam et ipsa scientia potestās est
∼ for knowledge too in itself is power.

1597 F. BACON *De Haeresibus* x.

nāscentēs morimur
∼ literally, 'from the moment of being born, we die', i.e. we begin the process of dying at the moment of our birth.

MANILIUS *Astronomica* iv.16.

nātāle solum
∼ native soil.

nātūra abhorret ā vacuō
∼ nature abhors a vacuum.

Cf. 1551 T. CRANMER *Answer to Gardiner* 299 Naturall reason aborreth vacuum.

nātūrae dēbitum reddidērunt
∼ they paid the debt of nature, i.e. they died.

CORNELIUS NEPOS *Vitae, De Regibus* i.5.

nātūram expellās furcā, tamen usque recurret
∼ even though you drive out nature with a pitchfork, yet she will always return.

HORACE *Epistles* I.x.24. Since nature will always win through, the poet's advice is to live according to her dictates, following the Stoic principle.

nāviget Anticyram
∼ let him sail to Anticyra.

HORACE *Satires* II.iii.166. The poet recommends this destination, a town on the northern side of the Gulf of Corinth in Greece, for the reckless man of ambition, for there hellebore could be found, a cure for madness.

Cf. 1561 T. NORTON *Institution of Christian religion* iv.xix. (1634) 730 [margin]
Anticyra where groweth Hellebor, a good purgation for phrenticke heads.

nē Aesōpum quidem trīvit
∿ he hasn't even thumbed Aesop, i.e. he is a total ignoramus.

nē cēde malīs
∿ do not give in to misfortunes.

See TU NE CEDE . . .

necessitās nōn habet lēgem
∿ necessity has no law.

Cf. 1377 LANGLAND *Piers Plowman* B.xx.10 Nede ne hath no lawe, ne neure
shal falle in dette.

Cf. 1680 *Kind Keeper* III.ii Necessity has no Law; I must be patient.

nec scīre fās est omnia
∿ to know all things is not permitted.

HORACE *Odes* IV.iv.22. The poet says that it is not right to try to unearth
every last detail, e.g., in this instance, why the Vindelici, an Alpine tribe,
use the Amazonian axe.

nec tēcum possum vīvere, nec sine tē
∿ I can neither live with you nor without you.

MARTIAL xii.46.

nefāstī diēs
∿ 'unlucky days'; days when no public business is permitted.

nē frontī crēde
∿ do not trust the face, i.e. do not trust appearances.

nēmine contrādīcente (abbreviated to nem. con.)
∿ with no one speaking in opposition.

1588 R. HOVENDEN in *Collect.* (O.H.S.) I.232 The Coll. flatly denied to grant
the Lease (*nem. con.*).

nēmine dissentiente (abbreviated to nem. diss.)
∿ with no one disagreeing.

1791 *Hist. Eur.* in *Ann. Reg.* 37/2 The lord chancellor put the question . . .
when it was declared that the contents had it *nem. diss.*

1991 *Weekly Law Rep.* 24 May 391 The motion was declared to be carried
nemine dissentiente. No doubt . . . [the] Council were extremely aggrieved
that they had to pass this motion.

nēmō ante mortem beātus

∼ no one (should be counted) happy before his/her death.

Based on OVID *Metamorphoses* iii.136–7. The poet here reproduces in Latin a common Greek sentiment.

nemo līber est quī corporī servit

∼ no one who is a slave to his body is free.

SENECA *Epistles* xcii.33.

nēmō mē impūne lacessit

∼ no one attacks me with impunity. The motto of the kings of Scotland and of the Order of the Thistle.

nēmō mortālium omnibus hōrīs sapit

∼ no mortal is wise at all times.

nēmō repente fit turpissimus

∼ no one has reached the lowest depths of baseness all at once.

JUVENAL ii.83. The poet puts the question, if you start with cross-dressing, where will you end up?

nē nimium

∼ not too much, i.e. avoid excess.

nē plūs ultrā

∼ literally, 'no further', the words are a prohibition of further advance or action; also an impassable obstacle or limitation; also the utmost limit to which one can go or has gone; the furthest point reached or capable of being reached.

The words were alleged to have been inscribed on the Pillars of Hercules (at the Straits of Gibraltar) to point out that ships sailing westwards out of the Mediterranean could go no further. Also found in the forms *non plus ultra* and *non ultra*. First recorded use in English 1661.

1760–72 H. BROOKE *Fool of Quality* (1792) II.81 The populace ... have arrived to their *ne plus ultra* of insolence.

1823 BYRON *Age of Bronze* xi The all-prolific land Of *ne plus ultra* ultras.

nē quid nimis

∼ (let there be) nothing in excess, i.e. avoid excess.

TERENCE *Andria* 61. This prohibition was inscribed in Greek on the temple of the god Apollo at Delphi.

nescit vōx missa revertī
~ a word once published cannot be recalled.

HORACE *Ars Poetica* 390. The poet suggests that you hang on to your work for nine years before publishing it. This will give you enough time for consultation and revision.

nē sūtor ultrā crepidam
~ let not the shoemaker go beyond his last (a wooden or metal model on which a shoemaker fashions shoes or boots).

ERASMUS *Adages* I.vi.16, based on *Pliny's Natural History* xxxv.85. The elder Pliny tells how a cobbler criticized the painting of a sandal in a work of Apelles, the most famous of Greek painters. When he went on to criticize the subject's legs, Apelles burst out with this response. This is the basis of the English proverb 'let the cobbler stick to his last'.

Note the English word *ultracrepidate* (= criticize ignorantly).

nihil ad rem
~ nothing to do with the point (in hand).

nihil obstat
~ nothing stands in the way.

nihil quod tetigit nōn ōrnāvit
~ he touched nothing without embellishing it.

Based on Samuel Johnson's epitaph on Oliver Goldsmith (1728–74). Cf. NULLUM QUOD TETIGIT . . .

nīl āctum credēns dum quid superesset agendum
~ thinking nothing done while anything was yet to do.

LUCAN ii.657. The poet comments on the energy of Caesar who thought he had achieved nothing until he had achieved everything.

nīl admīrārī
~ to wonder at nothing.

HORACE *Epistles* I.vi.1. The full quotation means: 'to wonder at nothing is just about the only way a man can become contented and remain so.' Hence the words can also refer to a person adopting this attitude.

1748 LORD CHESTERFIELD *Letter* 27 Sept. (1774) I.345 This book . . . will both divert and astonish you; and at the same time, teach you *nil admirari*.

1866 MRS GASKELL *Wives & Daughters* I.xxii.287 Every inflexion of the voice breathed out . . . admiration! And this from the *nil admirari* brother.

nīl dēspērandum
~ nothing to be despaired of, i.e. do not despair.

HORACE *Odes* I.vii.27. The full quotation means: 'no need to despair with Teucer as your leader and Teucer to protect you.' Teucer, banished by his father from his island of Salamis near Athens, tells his grieving companions not to despair while he is their leader. They shall found another Salamis (in Cyprus).

nīl igitur mors est ad nōs neque pertinet hīlum
~ death therefore is nothing to us and it concerns us not a scrap.

LUCRETIUS *De Rerum Natura* iii.830. The poet aims to free his readers from fear of something after death. When we die, it is extinction.

nīl mortālibus arduī est
~ for men no height is too steep.

HORACE *Odes* I.iii.37. The poet writes indignantly of the folly of men in their attempts to scale the heavens.

nīl nisi bonum *See* DE MORTUIS NIL NISI BONUM.

nimium nē crēde colōrī
~ do not trust too much to appearances.

VIRGIL *Eclogues* ii.17. Corydon, hopelessly in love with the beautiful Alexis, tells him not to bank too much on his complexion; but the words have a slightly different meaning out of context.

nisi Dominus, frūstrā
~ unless the Lord (build the house), it is in vain (to build it).

From the beginning of Psalm 127. The motto of Edinburgh.

nītimur in vetitum semper cupimusque negāta
~ we always strive after what is forbidden and desire what is denied us.

OVID *Amores* III.iv.17. The poet points out the dangers in trying to keep guard over a pretty girl.

nītor in adversum
~ I struggle against adverse circumstances.

OVID *Metamorphoses* ii.72. Apollo tells his son Phaethon that he has to drive the chariot of the sun in the opposite direction to the spinning vault of heaven. He is trying to dissuade Phaethon from insisting on driving it himself.

noctuās Athēnās ferre

∼ to carry owls to Athens, i.e. to carry coals to Newcastle.

Athens abounded with owls and the owl was the bird of its goddess Athene. To take owls there would be unnecessary and absurd.

nōlēns volēns

∼ unwilling or willing, whether willing or not.

1593 G. PEELE *The famous chronicle of King Edward the first* in *Works* [Routledge] 394/2 A little serves the friar's lust, When *nolens volens* fast I must.

nōlī mē tangere

∼ touch me not.

The words of Christ to Mary Magdalene after the Resurrection (John xx.17.1 in Vulgate). They are used of paintings of this scene, as well as metaphorically.

1680 J. EVELYN *Diary* 2 Sept. The *Noli me tangere of our blessed Saviour to Mary Magdalen after his Resurrection*, of Hans Holbein.

1822 J. DE QUINCEY *Confessions* 28 A sort of *noli me tangere* manner, nervously apprehensive of too familiar approach.

nōlle prōsequī

∼ literally, 'to be unwilling to pursue', an entry made upon the record of a court, when the plaintiff or prosecutor abandons part, or all, of his suit or prosecution against a defendant or defendants.

1681 LUTTRELL *A brief historical relation of state affairs* (1857) 1.70 A privy seal, commanding Mr. atturney generall to enter a nolle prosequi to the said indictment.

nōminātim

∼ 'by name', expressly.

1835 *U.S. Rep.* 34.732 To the king it mattered not whether the lands were conveyed to the house as a firm, or to the partners nominatim.

1982 *Land Q.Rev.* 98.383 Parliament authorized the appointment of a successor to Sir James Wigram, *nominatim*.

nōminātīvus pendēns

∼ a 'hanging nominative'.

First recorded use in English 1867.

1926 FOWLER *Modern English Usage* 611/2 Nominativus pendens.., A form of anacoluthon in which a sentence is begun with what appears to be the subject, but before the verb is reached something else is substituted in word or in thought, & the supposed subject is left in the air.

An example, from Shakespeare's *Richard III*, III.ii.58–9, is: '. . . they which brought me in my master's hate, I live to look upon their tragedy.'

nōminis umbra
~ the shadow of a name, a name without substance.

Cf. MAGNI NOMINIS UMBRA.

1856 W. BAGEHOT *National Review* Apr. 363 Taylor's theorem will go down to posterity, . . . but what does posterity know of the deceased Taylor? *Nominis umbra* is rather a compliment; for it is not substantial enough to have a shadow.

nōn amo tē, Sabidī, nec possum dīcere quārē
~ I do not love you, Sabidius, and I cannot say why.

MARTIAL I.xxxii.1. The next line means, 'All I can say is this, that I do not love you.' A famous imitation of these lines was written by Thomas Brown (1663–1704) about John Fell, Dean of Christ Church, Oxford:

I do not love you, Dr Fell,
But why I cannot tell;
But this I know full well,
I do not love you, Dr Fell.

nōn Anglī, sed angelī
~ not Angles (English), but angels.

The words of the future Pope Gregory in 573 when he saw some fair-haired Anglo-Saxon child slaves at Rome. It was this conversation that, according to tradition, inspired St Augustine to go to Britain in AD 597 to convert the country. (In fact Christianity had long been established in Britain.)

nōn bis in idem
~ literally, 'not twice for the same thing', i.e. no one can be tried for a second time on the same charge.

nōn compos mentis
~ not of sound mind.

nōn est vīvere sed valēre vīta est
~ life is not just to be alive but to be well.

MARTIAL VI.lxx.15.

nōn ignāra malī miserīs succurrere discō
~ not unschooled in disaster myself, I learn how to come to the help of the wretched.

VIRGIL *Aeneid* i.630. Dido, queen of Carthage, who has been through terrible sufferings herself, expresses her sympathetic willingness to help the apparently shipwrecked Trojans and their leader Aeneas.

nōn licet
~ it is not allowed.

nōn licet omnibus adīre Corinthum
~ not everyone is allowed to get to Corinth.

Based on HORACE *Epistles* I.xvii.36. The poet here renders a Greek proverb which means that 'the highest prizes are only on offer to the lucky few.' Corinth was notoriously expensive—with notoriously expensive courtesans—and thus its pleasures were not available to all comers.

nōn liquet
~ literally, 'it is not clear', i.e. the case is not clear.

First recorded use in English 1656.

1802 S. T. COLERIDGE *Unpublished Letter to J. P. Estlin* (Stanf.) 86 A non liquet concerning the nature and being of Christ.

nōn nōbīs, Domine
~ not unto us, O Lord.

The first words of Psalm 115, used as an expression of humble gratitude or thanksgiving for mercies vouchsafed: glory is not due to us but to God.

1475 *Mankind* 480 in *Macro Plays* 18 'Non nobis, domine; non nobis', by sent Deny!

nōn olet
~ it does not stink (said of money, no matter how unsavoury its source).

For the anecdote (SUETONIUS *Vespasian* xxiii) which gave rise to this saying, *see* LUCRI BONUS EST ODOR EX RE QUALIBET.

nōn omnia possumus omnēs
~ we cannot, all of us, do everything.

VIRGIL *Eclogues* viii.63. The poet expresses his awareness of his own limitations and calls upon the Muses to help him.

nōn omnis moriar
~ I shall not wholly die.

HORACE *Odes* III.xxx.6. The poet knows that he will die, but that his poetry will in a sense keep him alive.

nōn passibus aequīs
~ not with equal (that is, shorter) steps.

VIRGIL *Aeneid* ii.724. Aeneas is accompanied by his little son Ascanius as his family leaves Troy on the night of its sacking. The little boy scurries along beside his father with shorter steps.

nōn placet
~ it does not please, i.e. a negative vote.

1589 R. GREENE *Arcadia=Menaphon* (Arb.) 42 When I craued a finall resolution to my fatall passions, shee filde her . . . eyes full of furie, turned her backe, and shooke me off with a *Non placet*.

nōn plūs ultrā *See* NE PLUS ULTRA.

nōn scholae sed vītae discimus
~ we learn not for school but for life.

SENECA *Epistles* cvi.12.

nōn sequitur
~ it does not follow, i.e. an inference or a conclusion which does not follow from the premisses.

First recorded use in English 1564.

1855 G. ELIOT *Essays* (1884) 150 His practice is in many ways an amiable *non sequitur* from his teaching.

nōn sum quālis eram bonae sub rēgnō Cinarae
~ I'm not what I was under the rule of good Cinara.

HORACE *Odes* IV.i.3–4. The poet pleads with the goddess of love to stop tempting him. He's not as strong as he used to be.

nōn ultrā *See* NE PLUS ULTRA.

nōnum premātur in annum
~ keep (your work) back till the ninth year.

HORACE *Ars Poetica* 388. Horace advises the poet not to rush into publication!

nōn ut edam vīvō sed ut vīvam edō
~ I do not live to eat but I eat to live.

nōsce tē ipsum
∼ know thyself.

Based on CICERO *Tusculan Disputations* i.52. Cicero renders in Latin the famous motto (γνῶθι σεαυτόν) inscribed on the temple of Apollo at Delphi.

nōscitur ē sociīs
∼ he is known by his companions.

Cf. 1541 M. COVERDALE *Christen State of Matrymonye* tr. from H. Bullinger's F6 So maye much be spyed also, by the company and pastyme that a body vseth. For a man is for the mooste parte condicioned euen lyke vnto them that he kepeth company wythe all.

notā bene (abbreviated to N B)
∼ note well, take notice.

1721 M. PRIOR *Daphne & Apollo* 65 Next, nota bene, you shall never rove.

novus homō (plural novī hominēs)
∼ a new man, upstart, parvenu.

1589 T. SMITH *Commonwealth of England* i.xx.36 Those which were *novi homines*, were more allowed, for their vertues new and newly shewen, than the old smell of auncient race.

nūlla umquam dē morte hominis cūnctātio longa est
∼ when a human life is at stake, no delay is ever excessive.

JUVENAL vi.221.

nūllī secundus
∼ second to none.

1869 S. R. HOLE *Book about Roses* iv.55 If Mr. Shirley Hibberd . . . can grow good roses within four miles of the General Post-Office . . . it is quite certain that he would be *nulli secundus* with the full advantage of situation and soil.

nūllum magnum ingenium sine mixtūrā dēmentiae fuit
∼ there has been no great genius who did not have a spice of madness in him.

SENECA *Dialogi* IX.xvii.10. Seneca here quotes Aristotle. Cf. John Dryden, *Absalom and Achitophel* i.163: Great wits are sure to madness near alli'd . . .

nūllum (understand scrībendī genus) quod tetigit nōn ōrnāvit
∼ he touched no form of literature which he did not adorn.

Based on Samuel Johnson's Latin epitaph on Goldsmith, which means: 'To Oliver Goldsmith, poet, naturalist, and historian, who left hardly any form of writing untouched and touched none which he did not adorn.'

numerus clausus

∼ a closed or restricted number, i.e. a fixed maximum number of entrants admissible to an academic institution.

1925 *Nation* (N.Y.) 8 Apr. 374 The *numerus clausus*, driven out of Russia, still keeps eager Jewish youth from the learning they crave in Poland, Hungary, and Rumania.

nunc dīmittis

∼ now you send forth, an abbreviation of the first words of the Song of Simeon in Luke ii.29 ('Lord, now lettest thou thy servant depart in peace'); thus the canticle beginning with these words; also permission to leave life or some occupation.

1552 *Book of Common Prayer*, Evening Prayer Rubric After that, (*Nunc dimittis*) in Englishe, as foloweth.

1642 NETHERSOLE *Consid. upon Affairs* 8 I should ... cheerfully sing my *Nunc dimittis*.

nunc est bibendum

∼ now it is time to drink.

HORACE *Odes* I.xxxvii.1 The poet urges joyful celebration now that the vile Cleopatra, the queen of Egypt and the enemy of Rome, is dead. The ode ends, however, with a poignantly sympathetic estimate of Cleopatra's noble end. Nothing in her life became her like the leaving it.

nunc stāns

∼ literally, 'standing now', the eternal timeless 'now' presumed, as an attribute of God, to be co-existent with Time.

1651 T. HOBBES *Leviathan* xlvi.374 But they will teach us that Eternity is the Standing still of the Present Time, a *Nunc-stans* (as the Schools call it;) which neither they, nor any else understand.

nunc vīnō pellite cūrās

∼ now drive away your sorrows with wine.

HORACE *Odes* I.vii.31. Expelled from the island of Salamis by his father, Teucer, awash with wine, exhorts his followers with these words.

nunquam minus sōlus quam cum sōlus
~ never less alone than when alone.

Based on CICERO *De Republica* i.27. When one is absorbed in one's studies, solitude is no burden.

nunquam nōn parātus
~ never unprepared.

obiit

∼ he/she died.

Found on tombstones and in church records with the date of the death.

obiter dictum (plural obiter dicta)

∼ literally, '(a thing) said by the way', an incidental statement or remark.

1812 *Edinburgh Review* XIX.302 It was more of an *obiter dictum* than of a point ruled.

obscūrum per obscūrius

∼ (explaining) the unclear by means of the more unclear, an unclear argument or proposition (expressed) in terms of one that is even less clear.

1616 W. CLERK *Withal's Dictionary of English & Latin* (rev. edn.) 574 *Obscurum per obscurius*. I am as wise as I was before.

1952 G. SARTON *A history of science* I.viii.200 Herodotus ... was already combining Pythagorean ideas with Egyptian, Orphic, and Bacchic ones, and he mixed up the story of Pythagoras with that of Zalmoxis, thus explaining *obscurum per obscurius*.

obstā prīncipiīs

∼ resist at the beginning.

OVID *Remedium Amoris* 91. If you don't stamp out the disease of love at the start, you are lost.

occasiōnem cognōsce

∼ recognize an opportunity, i.e. strike while the iron is hot.

occultae inimīcitiae magis timendae sunt quam apertae

∼ hidden hostilities are more to be feared than open ones.

Based on CICERO *In Verrem* II.v.182.

ōderint dum metuant
~ let them hate (me) provided that they fear (me).

ACCIUS *Atreus* fragment 4, quoted in CICERO *Philippic* i.14. Atreus' espousal of this attitude did not save him from being murdered by his nephew Aegisthus. The emperor Caligula often quoted this line (SUETONIUS *Caligula* xxx.1): he too was murdered. His predecessor Tiberius adapted the words to 'Let them hate me as long as they respect me' (SUETONIUS *Tiberius* lix.2).

ōdī et amō
~ I hate and I love.

CATULLUS lxxxv.1. The poet memorably expresses the torture of conflicting emotions: 'I hate and I love. Perhaps you ask why I experience this. I do not know, but I feel it happening and I am in torment.'

ōdī profānum vulgus et arceō
~ I hate the uninitiated crowd and keep clear of it.

HORACE *Odes* III.i.1. The poet, priest of the Muses, here uses priestly language. When quoted in English, the words express a resolution to avoid the common rabble, but this is something of a distortion of the meaning of the Latin. Horace is insisting on his special status as a poet.

odium theologicum
~ the hatred of theologians (in controversy), i.e. the hatred which proverbially characterizes theological dissensions.

The following adjectives are also used with the word *odium* to refer to such hatred in other spheres: *academicum* (academic), *aestheticum* (aesthetic), *archaeologicum* (archaeological), *biologicum* (biological), *ethicum* (ethical), *medicum* (medical), *musicum* (musical), *philologicum* (philological), *philosophicum* (philosophical), *scholasticum* (scholarly).

1673 J. FLAVEL *Fountain of Life* xxx.414 Strigelius desired to die, that he might be freed *ab implacabilibus odiis theologorum*, from the implacable strifes of contending Divines.

ō fortūnātam nātam mē cōnsule Rōmam
~ O happy Rome, born for my consulship!

CICERO *Poems* fragment xii.1. A much-ridiculed line from Cicero's notorious poem about his own consulship in 63 BC when he saved the state from Catiline's conspiracy. However mocked as a poet he has proved to be, Cicero none the less smoothed out the Latin hexameter line and established the pattern employed by Virgil, Ovid, and their successors.

ō fortūnātōs nimium, sua sī bona nōrint, agricolās
~ o too happy farmers, if they but knew their luck.

VIRGIL *Georgics* ii.458. Virgil celebrates the blessings of the life of the farmer, who avoids the horrors of war and is the beneficiary of the bountiful earth.

ohē! iam satis
~ hold! that's enough already.

HORACE *Satires* I.v.12–13. Are the boatmen trying to cram too many passengers onto a barge?

olet lucernā
~ it smells of the lamp.

Used of a literary work, these words suggest that the toil devoted to it (in midnight labours by lamplight) is only too evident: it *appears* laboured.

ōlim
~ at one time, formerly.

First recorded use in English 1645.

1975 *Times Literary Supplement* 28 Nov. 1423/1 The former colonial archive at Jakarta (*olim* Batavia).

ō mātre pulchrā fīliā pulchrior *See* MATRE PULCHRA FILIA PULCHRIOR.

ō mihi praeteritōs referat sī Iuppiter annōs
~ o, if only Jupiter could restore to me the years gone by.

VIRGIL *Aeneid* viii.560. The Arcadian king Evander wishes that he could be young again so that he himself could fight and not be compelled to send his son Pallas to war on his behalf. His forebodings are fulfilled: Pallas is killed.

ō miserās hominum mentēs, ō pectora caeca!
~ o wretched minds of men, o their blind hearts!

LUCRETIUS *De Rerum Natura* ii.14. The philosophical poet exclaims in sadness over those involved in the madding crowd's ignoble strife. If only they would devote themselves to the tenets of Epicurus.

omne ignōtum prō magnificō
~ whatever is unknown is held to be magnificent.

TACITUS *Agricola* 30. A British leader is trying to explain to his men why the Romans wish to conquer Scotland.

omnem crēde diem tibi dīlūxisse suprēmum
~ believe every day to have dawned to be your last.

HORACE *Epistles* I.iv.13. Horace advises his fellow poet Tibullus to follow an Epicurean life-style, making the most of every day. *See* CARPE DIEM.

omnēs ūna manet nox
~ one night awaits (us) all.

HORACE *Odes* I.xxviii.15. The poet puts these words in the mouth of a drowned man, who proceeds to ask a passing sailor to scatter some sand on his corpse.

omne tulit pūnctum quī miscuit ūtile dulcī
~ he has carried every vote who has mixed the useful with the pleasing.

HORACE *Ars Poetica* 343. Horace advises the poet to combine the educative with the enjoyable.

1871–2 G. ELIOT *Middlemarch* xxxiv [he] remembers what the right quotations are, *omne tulit punctum* and that sort of thing ...

omne vīvum ex ovō
~ every living thing comes from an egg.

Attributed to William Harvey (1578–1650), the English physician who discovered the circulation of the blood. The first edition of Harvey's *De Generatione Animalium* (1651) has a frontispiece with an engraving of the god Jupiter holding an egg from the two halves of which various creatures—bird, snake, spider, child, etc.—are spilling out; the inscription on the egg reads *ex ovo omnia* (all from an egg). This was taken by early commentators to be Harvey's own saying, but from the eighteenth century onwards it has commonly been misquoted as *omne vivum ex ovo* (or even *omne animale ex ovo*), which in fact misrepresents Harvey's point.

omnia bona bonīs
~ all things are good to the good.

omnia mūtantur, nōs et mūtāmur in illīs
~ all things are in the process of change, we also are in the process of change among them.

See TEMPORA MUTANTUR ...

omnia vincit amor, et nōs cēdāmus amōrī
~ love conquers all things, let us too yield to love.

VIRGIL *Eclogues* x.69. Chaucer's Prioress (General Prologue to the *Canterbury Tales*, 161–2) wears a brooch 'On which ther was first write a crowned A, And after *Amor vincit omnia*.'

omnia vincit labor
~ labour conquers all. *See* LABOR OMNIA VINCIT.

omnium gatherum
~ a gathering of all (sorts); a miscellaneous assemblage, collection, or mixture (of persons or things); a confused medley.

Gatherum is a mock-Latin word from 'gather'.

1530 CROKE *Letter to Cranmer* (MS. Cott. Vit. B xiii.123 b) Certayne subscriptions unto the kynge, wheroff sauff ij, there ys none worthe a botton, but be omnium gatherum.

onus probandī
~ the burden of proof, the obligation under which one who makes an assertion, allegation, or charge is of proving the same.

1722 *Act Encour. Silk Manuf.* in *London Gazette* no. 6040/5 The Onus Probandi shall lie on the Exporter, Claimer, or Owner thereof.

opere citātō (abbreviated to op. cit.)
~ in the work quoted.

1883 *Nineteenth Century* Feb. 213 *Op. cit.* vol. ii. pp. 200, 201.

optimīs parentibus
~ to my excellent parents.

A not uncommon formula for the dedication of a book.

optimum est patī quod ēmendāre nōn possīs
~ it is best to endure what you cannot put right.

SENECA *Epistles* cvii.9. What can't be cured must be endured.

opus alexandrīnum
~ literally, 'Alexandrian work', a type of pavement mosaic work consisting of coloured stone, glass, and semiprecious stones arranged in intricate geometric patterns.

It was much used in Byzantium in the ninth century and later in Italy.

opus artificem probat
~ the craftsman is known by (the quality of) his work.

136

opus Deī
~ the work of God; hence the Divine Office, or liturgical worship in general, seen as man's primary duty to God; and also (with capital initials) the name of a Roman Catholic organization of laymen and priests founded in Spain in 1928 with the purpose of re-establishing Christian ideals in society through the implementation of them in the lives of its members.

opus rēticulātum
~ literally, 'work patterned like a net', i.e. masonry arranged in squares or diamonds so that the mortar joints make a network pattern.

opus sectile
~ literally 'cut work', i.e. a form of floor decoration dating from Roman times and made up of pieces shaped individually to fit the pattern or design, in which respect it differs from mosaic which is an arrangement of regularly shaped pieces.

1852 *Murray's Handbook Northern Italy* (edn. 4) 490/1 This Florentine mosaic seems to be the 'opus sectile' of the Romans.

ōrā et labōrā
~ worship and work.

ōrā prō nōbīs
~ pray for us.

ōrātiō oblīqua ōrātiō rēcta
~ indirect speech/direct speech.

1842 W. E. JELF *Grammar of Greek Language* II.iv.508 The infin. and acc. follows the verb in the *oratio obliqua*, and then follows a dependent clause in which the verb stands in the *oratio recta*.

ōrātor fit, poēta nāscitur
~ the orator is made, the poet is born.

ōre rotundō
~ with round, full voice (literally, 'mouth').

HORACE *Ars Poetica* 323. The poet says that this is a gift of the Muses to the Greeks.

1720 J. SWIFT *Letter* 1 Dec. in *Works* (1859) II.300/1 Is taught there to mouth it gracefully, and to swear, as he reads French, *ore rotundo*.

ō sāncta simplicitās *See* SANCTA SIMPLICITAS.

ō sī sīc omnēs!
~ Oh, if only everyone was like this!

ō sī sīc omnia!
~ Oh, if only things were always like this!

ō tempora! o mōres!
~ What times! What customs!

CICERO *In Catilinam* i.2. This is an oft-quoted expression used to convey the lamentable decline which has led to degenerate modern times.

ōtium cum dignitāte
~ leisure with dignity.

CICERO *De Oratore* I.i.1.

ovem lupō committere
~ to entrust the sheep to the wolf, i.e. to take an action which is sure to lead to disaster.

Based on TERENCE *Eunuchus* 832.

P

pāce tuā
~ with your consent.

pacta sunt servanda
~ literally, 'agreements must be kept', i.e. the principle, especially in international law, that agreements are binding and inviolable.

Based on CICERO *De Officiis* III.xcii.

1855 R. PHILLIMORE *Commentaries upon International Law* II.v.vi.56 *Pacta sunt servanda* is the pervading maxim of International, as it was of Roman jurisprudence.

Paete, nōn dolet
~ Paetus, it doesn't hurt.

PLINY *Letters* III.xvi.6. Condemned to death on a charge of disloyalty by the emperor Nero, Caecina Paetus had to commit suicide. To give him the courage to do this, his wife Arria stabbed herself fatally and then handed Paetus the dagger with these 'almost immortal' words.

pallida mors aequō pulsat pede pauperum tabernās rēgumque turrēs
~ pale death kicks with impartial foot at the hovels of the poor and the towers of kings (*translation by David West*).

HORACE *Odes* I.iv.13–14. Death awaits us all, says the poet, and so we must make the most of the present.

palmam qui meruit ferat
~ let him who has won the palm wear it.

DR JORTIN *Lusus Poetici* viii.20.

pānem et circēnsēs
~ literally, 'bread and the circus', food and amusement.

JUVENAL x.81. The poet remarks scathingly that these are the only two interests of the Roman mob.

parcere subiectīs et dēbellāre superbōs
~ to spare the conquered and to fight the proud into submission.

VIRGIL *Aeneid* vi.854. This is a resonantly 'Roman' line. Dryden translates it, 'To tame the proud, the fetter'd slave to free.' This instruction, given to Aeneas by the ghost of his father Anchises in the underworld, is ignored by the hero at the end of the poem when he kills the Italian prince Turnus who kneels in submission at his feet.

parēns patriae
~ literally, 'parent of the country', i.e. the sovereign, or some other authority, regarded as the guardian or protector of citizens who are unable to protect themselves.

First recorded use in English 1764.

1883 *Wharton's Law Lexicon* (edn. 7) 593/2 *Parens patriae*, the sovereign, as *parens patriae*, has a kind of guardianship over various classes of persons, who, from their legal disability, stand in need of protection, such as infants, idiots, and lunatics.

parēs cum paribus facillimē congregantur
~ like most easily consorts with like, i.e. birds of a feather flock together.

CICERO *De Senectute* iii. Cicero quotes this as an 'old proverb'.

parī passū
~ with equal pace, at the same speed, side by side.

1567 SIR N. THROKMORTON *Letter* in Robertson *Hist. Scot. Wks.* (1826) I.378 (note) They think it convenient to proceed with yow both for a while *pari passu*.

1890 GLADSTONE *Sp. Ho. Commons* 19 Feb. The only method of describing *pari passu* was that adopted by Mr. John Bright . . . when he said that, when people were content with a *pari passu* progress, it was like driving six omnibuses abreast down Park-lane.

pār nōbile frātrum
~ a noble pair of brothers.

HORACE *Satires* II.iii.243. The context makes this a scornful appellation. These brothers were twins in their decadent tastes and lunched on vastly expensive nightingales.

pars prō tōtō

~ literally, 'the part for the whole', i.e. a part considered as representative of the whole.

First recorded use in English 1702.

1965 *English Studies* XLVI.55 It is a *pars pro toto* figure, just as *rand* is used to refer not only to the metal border or ring round the wooden board but also to the shield as such.

particeps crīminis (plural unchanged or participēs crīminis)

~ accomplice or partner in crime.

1634 E. COKE *Institutes* (1644) III.lxiv.138 All agree, that procurors of such treason to be done before the fact done, if after the fact be done accordingly, in case of treason, are principals, for that they are *participes criminis* in the very act of counterfeiting.

1983 *Southern Reporter* 435 145 We are pleased to state that it was apparently understood by all concerned that the wife was not in particeps criminis in the act of burglary by defendant.

parturiunt montēs, nascētur rīdiculus mūs

~ the mountains will labour and bring to birth a comical mouse (*translation by Niall Rudd*).

HORACE *Ars Poetica* 139. If you begin your poem in the grand old epic style, there is a great danger that you will not be able to keep it up. This will lead to bathos, a figure of speech which Horace memorably illustrates in this line.

parva compōnere magnīs

~ to compare small things to great.

VIRGIL *Georgics* iv.176. The poet here likens the metal-working giants, the Cyclopes, to the tiny bees to which the last book of his poem about farming is largely given over. Both giants and bees labour collectively and constructively.

parva levēs capiunt animōs

~ small things fascinate trivial minds.

OVID *Ars Amatoria* i.159. Ovid is recommending trivial courtesies, such as plumping out a cushion for her, which can often advance one's progress with a woman at the races.

Cf. 1973 *Galt Toy Catalogue* 35 As the saying goes—Little things please little minds.

passim

~ everywhere, all through.

This Latin word is used chiefly after the name of a book or author, to indicate the occurrence of something in various places throughout the book or writings. First recorded use in English 1803.

1821 BYRON *Don Juan* III.cxi I'll prove that such the opinion of the critic is,
From Aristotle *passim*.

pater historiae
∼ the father of history.

CICERO *De Legibus* I.i.5. Cicero here refers to the Greek historian Herodotus (*c.* 490–*c.* 425 BC) who, in his account of the Persian Wars at the start of the fifth century BC, wrote on a scale which had never been attempted before.

Pater Noster
∼ Our Father.

The opening of the Lord's Prayer in Latin.

pater patriae
∼ father of the fatherland.

This title was conferred on Cicero, Caesar, and Augustus, the first Roman emperor. Tiberius, Augustus' heir, never accepted it, but all subsequent emperors took the title if they lived long enough.

patris est filius
∼ he is his father's son, i.e. like father, like son.

paucis verbis
∼ in few words.

paulo maiora canamus
∼ let us sing of things which are a little more important.

VIRGIL *Eclogues* iv.1. Virgil here employs litotes ('a little more important' means vastly so) to launch a far grander poem than the first three eclogues.

pauper ubique iacet
∼ the poor man everywhere lies low.

OVID *Fasti* i.218. The poet complains that in today's Rome money counts for everything. The poor man doesn't stand a chance.

pax
∼ peace; also (in schoolboy slang) 'Keep quiet!', 'Truce!'.

Found in such expressions as *pax Romana* and *pax Americana* where the existence of peace within the sphere controlled by Rome and America is referred to.

1852–82 ROGET *Thesaurus* para. 403 *Silence . . . int.* hush! silence! soft! whist! tush! chut! tut! pax!

pāx vōbīs(cum)!
~ peace (be) with you!

1593 G. PEELE *The famous chronicle of King Edward the first* in *Works*. 381/2 *Pax vobis, Pax vobis!* good fellows, fair fall ye.

peccā fortiter
~ sin strongly.

M. LUTHER *Letter to Melanchthon* 1 Aug. 1521 (in *Epistolae*, Jenna (1556) i.345). The context of this is a sentence meaning, 'Be a sinner and sin strongly, but more strongly have faith and rejoice in Christ.'

peccāvī
~ I have sinned.

An acknowledgement or confession of guilt. Midas exclaims this (in the plural) at *Metamorphoses* ii.132 when repenting of his choice of gift from Bacchus, the 'Midas touch' which turns everything to gold. There is an anecdote, no longer believed but *se non è vero, è molto ben trovato* (if it is not true, it is a very happy invention), about Sir Charles Napier who, after winning the battle of Hyderabad (then in north-west India) in 1843, sent the one-word message *peccavi* to his superiors. He meant not 'I have sinned' but 'I have (i.e. have conquered) Sind', a region in that area.

pectus est quod disertōs facit
~ it is the heart that makes men eloquent.

QUINTILIAN *Institutio Oratoria* X.vii.15.

penātēs
~ the guardian deities of the Roman household and of the state, who were worshipped in the interior of every house.

See also LARES ET PENATES.

1513 G. DOUGLAS *Aeneis* XIII.x.81 Penates, or the Goddis domesticall.

pendente līte
~ while a suit is pending, i.e. during litigation.

A Latin phrase of the Roman Law. First recorded use in English 1726.

1973 N. Y. *Law Journal* 31 Aug. 18/3 The cross motion for an order for renewal of plaintiff's motion for alimony pendente lite is denied, no sufficiently persuasive ground in support of same having been demonstrated.

per ardua ad astra
~ through difficulties to the stars.

The motto of the Royal Air Force.

per annum
~ by the year, every year, yearly.

Almost always in reference to a sum of money paid or received.

1601 R. JOHNSON *Botero's (G.) The Worlde, or . . . the most famous kingdomes and commonweales therein* (1603) 89 The professor in divinity, hath per annum 1125 florens.

per capita (plural; singular per caput)
~ literally, 'by heads', i.e. individually. The singular form is far less frequently used.

per centum
~ on each hundred, i.e. per cent.

per contrā
~ on the opposite side (of an account, etc.); on the other hand.

1554 W. PRAT *The discription of the contrey of Aphrique* Ep. A v b Honour . . . doth the noble man ateyne; which . . . preferreth and advanceth his pore servauntes; *per contra* in how much displeasure with God, . . . doth he incur in whose servyce his poore servantes do not floryshe.

per diem
~ by the day, daily.

First recorded use in English 1520.

1742 H. FIELDING *Joseph Andrews* I.viii To attend twice *per diem* at the polite churches and chapels.

pereant quī ante nōs nostra dīxērunt
~ perish those who have said our (good) things before us.

Attributed to Donatus, a scholar of the fourth century AD, and to St Augustine.

perfervidum ingenium Scotōrum
~ the intense earnestness of Scotsmen.

1849 R. BUCHANAN *The ten year's conflict, being the history of the disruption of the Church of Scotland* xvi.51.

perfer, obdūrā

~ hold out, be strong.

CATULLUS viii.11. The poet tries to tell himself to stand firm in his resistance to a hopeless love affair.

per mēnsem

~ by the month, monthly.

1647 *Kingd. Weekly Intelligencer* no. 238.758 The addition of forty thousand pounds *per mensem* to the present sixty thousand pounds.

permitte dīvīs cētera

~ leave the rest to the gods.

HORACE *Odes* I.ix.9. When it is bitterly cold outside, pile up logs on the fire and drink vintage wine. Leave everything else to the gods. This is from one of the many poems in which Horace urges his addressee to make the most of the present and not to ask what will happen tomorrow.

perpetuum mōbile

~ perpetual motion.

1688 R. CUDWORTH *Treatise of Freewill* (1838) 28 This is an ever bubbling fountain in the centre of the soul, an elater or spring of motion, both a *primum* and a *perpetuum mobile* in us, the first wheel that sets all the other wheels in motion, and an everlasting and incessant mover.

per sē

~ by itself; intrinsically, essentially; without reference to anything (or any one) else.

First recorded use in English 1572.

1606 SHAKESPEARE *Troilus & Cressida* I.ii.15 They say he is a very man *per se* and stands alone.

persōna (plural persōnae)

~ a character assumed or acted.

1909 E. POUND (title) Personae.

1963 W. H. AUDEN *Dyer's Hand* 401 The more closely his [sc. Byron's] poetic *persona* comes to resemble the epistolary *persona* of his letters to his male friends ... the more authentic his poetry seems.

1976 *Gramophone* Dec. 965/3 George Logan and Patric Fyffe in the *personae* of Dr Evadne Hinge and Dame Hilda Bracket are on EMI One-Up OU2125 (7/76).

persōna grāta

~ an acceptable person; originally applied to a diplomatic

representative who is personally acceptable to the personage or government to which he is accredited.

1882 *Standard* 20 Dec. 5 At a supper of criminals in full work in their profession he might be welcomed as a *persona grata*.

persōna nōn grāta
~ the opposite of *persona grata*.

per variōs casūs, per tot discrīmina rērum
~ through many a mischance, through such a number of perilous events.

VIRGIL *Aeneid* i.204. Inwardly demoralized, Aeneas puts a brave face on it as he comforts his band of Trojan refugees over the many dangers they have passed.

petītiō prīncipiī
~ literally, 'begging or taking for granted of the beginning or of a principle', i.e. a logical fallacy which consists in taking for granted a premiss which is either equivalent to, or itself depends on, the conclusion, and requires proof; an instance of this; a 'begging the question'.

1531 W. TINDALE *Exposition of 1 John* v.1–3 in *Works* (1573) 420/1 Which kynde of disputyng schole men call *Petitio principii*, the prouyng of two certaine thynges, eche by the other, and is no prouyng at all.

pictor ignōtus
~ painter unknown.

pīnxit
~ he/she painted (it).

An engraving of a painting may well give the name of the painter in conjunction with this Latin word.

placet
~ it pleases.

See NON PLACET.

plēnō iūre
~ with full right, with full authority.

plūrēs crāpula quam gladius
~ drunkenness (finishes off) more people than the sword.

poëta nāscitur, nōn fit

$\sim$ the poet is born, not made.

Cf. ORATOR FIT, POETA NASCITUR.

pōns asinōrum

$\sim$ literally, 'bridge of asses': a humorous name for the fifth proposition of the first book of Euclid, from the difficulty which beginners or dull-witted persons find in 'getting over' or mastering it.

Hence also allusively.

1751 T. SMOLLETT *The adventures of Peregrine Pickle* I.xviii.138 Peregrine . . . began to read Euclid . . . but he had scarce advanced beyond the *Pons Asinorum*, when his ardor abated.

1845 R. FORD *Handbook for travellers in Spain* i.217/2 This bridge was the *pons asinorum* of the French, which English never suffered them to cross.

populus vult dēcipī, ergō dēcipiātur

$\sim$ the public wishes to be taken in, therefore let it be taken in.

Ascribed to Cardinal Carlo Caraffa, the morally worthless nephew and adviser of Pope Paul IV (Pope 1555–9). The draconian repressiveness of this violently reactionary Pope proved so little to the people's liking that on his death there was a popular riot and his statue on the Roman Capitol was toppled and mutilated.

poscimur

$\sim$ we are called on (to sing, etc.).

posse (abbreviation of **posse comitātūs**)

$\sim$ literally, 'the force of the county', the body of men above the age of fifteen in a county whom the sheriff may summon to repress a riot or for other purposes; also a body of men actually so raised and commanded by the sheriff.

1626 BACON (J.) The posse comitatus, the power of the whole county, is legally committed unto him.

possunt quia posse videntur

$\sim$ they can, because they think they can.

VIRGIL *Aeneid* v.231. The captain and crew of a ship in a ship race, having once begun to believe that they can win, are given the ability to win by that belief. (In fact they come second.)

post bellum

$\sim$ after the war.

1874 *Southern Magazine* XIV.37 It [sc. Atlanta] looks so little like a *post-bellum* town.

post coitum
~ after sexual intercourse.

post coitum omne animal trīste est
~ after sexual intercourse every animal is sad.

The phrase does not occur in classical Latin but derives from [Aristotle] *Problems* 877 b 9 and Pliny *Natural History* X.lxxxiii.

1762 L. STERNE *Tristram Shandy* V.xxxvi.126 The oily and balsamous parts are of a lively heat and spirit, which accounts for the observation of Aristotle, '*Quod omne animal post coitum est triste.*'

post equitem sedet ātra cūra
~ behind the horseman sits black care.

HORACE *Odes* III.i.40. Even a pleasure such as riding is clouded by the fear of an accident.

post factum
~ after the event.

1692 J. LOCKE *Some Considerations of . . . the value of money* 12 Unless you intend to break in only upon Mortgages and Contracts already made, and (which is not to be supposed) by a Law, *post factum*, void Bargains lawfully made.

post hoc, ergō propter hoc
~ after this, therefore on account of this; expressing the fallacy that a thing which follows another is therefore caused by it.

1704 J. NORRIS *An essay towards the theory of the ideal or intelligible world* II.iii.221 That maxim, '*Post hoc, ergo propter hoc,*' which indeed is good logick with the vulgar, . . . methinks should not pass for such with the learned.

post merīdiem (abbreviated to p.m.)
~ after midday.

post mortem
~ literally, 'after death'; (as a noun, usually hyphenated) an autopsy.

post nūbila, Phoebus
~ after clouds, the sun.

Phoebus was the sun god.

post obitum
~ after death.

post partum
~ after childbirth.

First recorded use in English 1844.

1929 *American Journal of Psychiatry* VIII.767 I didn't study the infanticidal impulses of many women, because these impulses are more prominent in post-partum depressions.

post scrīptum (abbreviated to **PS**)
~ written later, i.e. a postscript, often at the foot of a letter.

potius sērō quam nunquam
~ better late than never.

LIVY iv.2. The historian quotes the consuls as saying that now—better late than never—is the time to make a stand against the common people and their tribune Canuleius.

praemonitus, praemūnītus
~ forewarned, forearmed.

Cf. *c.* 1425 J. ARDERNE *Treatises of Fistula* (EETS) 22 He that is warned afore is noght bygiled.

prīmā faciē
~ at first sight; on the face of it.

1420 J. LYDGATE (?) *Assembly of Gods* 157 Here, prima facie, to vs he doth apere That he hath offendyd—no man can sey nay.

prīma inter parēs
~ first among her equals.

prīmum mōbile
~ literally, 'first moving thing': thus, the supposed outermost sphere (at first reckoned the ninth, later the tenth), added in the Middle Ages to the Ptolemaic system of astronomy, and supposed to revolve round the earth from east to west in twenty-four hours, carrying with it the (eight or nine) contained spheres.

1391 CHAUCER *Astrolabe* i. para. 17 This equinoxial is cleped the gyrdelle of the firste Moeuyng, or elles of the *angulus primi motus vel primi mobilis*.

prīmus inter parēs
~ first among equals.

prō [and] contrā, prō et contrā (abbreviated to prō [and] con, pro ēt con)

~ (arguments) for and against (*et* = and)

1426 J. LYDGATE *De Guileville's Pilgrimage* 5663 I tauhte folkys to argue Pro & contra, yong & olde.

prō ārīs et focīs

~ for altars and hearths; for the sake of, or on behalf of, religion and home.

First recorded use in English 1621.

1741 D. HUME *Essays, moral and political* iv.48 I wou'd only perswade Men not to contend, as if they were fighting *pro aris & focis*.

probātum est

~ it has been proved.

1573–80 G. HARVEY *Letter-book* (Camden) 138 By ye masse all, all is nawght, Probatum est; I teach as I am tawght.

probitās laudātur et alget

~ honesty is praised and left out in the cold.

JUVENAL i.74. The poet observes bitterly that crime pays.

prō bonō pūblicō

~ for the public good.

First recorded use in English 1726. Colloquially often shortened to *pro bono*. Hence (originally in United States usage), as an adjective, meaning legal work undertaken at no charge for a person unable to pay fees; also a lawyer who undertakes such work.

1922 J. JOYCE *Ulysses* 306 Someone ... ought to write a letter *pro bono publico* to the newspapers about the muzzling order for a dog the like of that.

1995 *Times* 19 Dec. 33/1 It is hoped that it may prompt lawyers to dig into their pockets or do more *pro bono* work.

procul, ō procul este, profānī!

~ far hence, o far hence, be ye, ye profane!

VIRGIL *Aeneid* vi.258. As Aeneas is about to descend to the underworld, the priestess who is to be his guide excludes the uninitiated from the ritual.

profānum vulgus

~ the common herd.

See ODI PROFANUM VULGUS ET ARCEO.

prō fōrmā
∼ as a matter of form, in the way of a formality.

A *pro forma* invoice is an invoice sent to a purchaser in advance of the ordered goods, so that formalities may be completed.

prō hāc vice
∼ for this occasion (only).

prō memoriā
∼ for a memorial.

prō nunc
∼ for now, for the present.

propāgandā fidē
∼ for extending the faith.

prō patriā
∼ for (one's) native land.

proprium hūmānī ingeniī est ōdisse quem laeseris
∼ it is characteristic of human nature to hate a man you have harmed.

TACITUS *Agricola* xlii. The historian offers this as an explanation for the emperor Gaius' hatred of the virtuous general, Agricola, who was incidentally Tacitus' father-in-law.

prō ratā
∼ in proportion to the value or extent (of his/her interest), proportionally.

1545 *Register of the Privy Council of Scotland* II.468 To mak payment of their part of the said taxatioun pro rata.

prōsit!
∼ may it benefit.

The word is used to wish good health, success, etc., especially as a toast in German-speaking countries.

prō tempore (abbreviated to **prō tem.**)
∼ for the time being, temporary.

First recorded use in English 1468.

1835 C. DICKENS *Letters* (ed. M. House)? 30 Oct. I.85 Through the stupidity of Frisby who was in attendance pro: tem: Frank Ross 'dropped in' to my writing room.

proximē accessit

~ literally, 'he she has come very near (or next)', a phrase indicating that the person in question has obtained the next place in merit to the actual winner of a prize, scholarship, etc.; hence (as a noun) the person him/herself or his/her position.

If more than one person has come second, the phrase changes to **proximē accessērunt** (they have come very near (or next)).

1878 L. LOCKHART *Mine is Thine* I.xi.224 I . . . was *proxime accessit* for the Chancellor's medal at Cambridge.

pulvis et umbra sumus

~ we are ashes and a shadow.

HORACE *Odes* IV.vii.16. Enjoy life to the full. When we are dead 'we are dust and dreams' (A. E. Housman's version).

Pūnica fidēs

~ Punic (Carthaginian) faith, i.e. treachery.

This was the Roman view of the trustworthiness of their most dangerous enemy. In his *Cato*, Addison writes: 'Our Punic faith Is infamous, and branded as a proverb.' *See also* FIDES PUNICA.

purpureus pannus

~ a purple patch.

HORACE *Ars Poetica* 15–16. This refers to a piece of fine writing sewn on to a work to make a striking effect.

putō deus fīō

~ I think I am becoming a god.

The words of the emperor Vespasian when fatally ill, quoted in SUETONIUS *Vespasian* xxiii.4.

QED

See QUOD ERAT DEMONSTRANDUM.

quā

~ in so far as, in the capacity of.

1647 N. WARD *The simple cobler of Aggawam in America* 56 Every man was as good a man as your Selfe, *qua* man.

quae nocent docent

~ things that injure teach.

quaere vērum

~ seek the truth.

quālis artifex pereō

~ what an artist I die!

The last words of the artistic Roman emperor Nero at his assassination in AD 68 are quoted in SUETONIUS *Nero* xlix.1.

quālis rēx, tālis grex

~ literally, 'as the ruler is, so is the flock', i.e. the leader sets the standard which his followers adopt.

Based on PETRONIUS *Satyricon* lviii.4: 'as the master, so too the slave.'

quantum meruit

~ as much as he has deserved, i.e. a reasonable sum of money to be paid for services rendered or work done, when the amount due is not determined by any provision of a legally enforceable contract.

1657 H. GRIMSTON tr. G. Croker's *Rep.* (Charles I) 77 It is the usuall way to lay down in certainty, *viz.* That he should pay for it *tantum quantum meruit, &c.,* and then to averre what it is reasonably worth, which being the common course and alwaies allowed, Judgment was therefore affirmed.

quantum mūtātus ab illō

~ how changed from him!, i.e. changed from the person you once were.

VIRGIL *Aeneid* ii.274. Aeneas sees the blood-boltered ghost of his fellow Trojan Hector in a dream and exclaims over how unlike he now is to the Hector who came back from the battlefield clad in the armour of his enemy Achilles.

quantum sufficit

~ as much as suffices, enough.

1699 *Honour of Gout* in Hart. *Misc.* (1809) II.45 We lead sedentary lives, feed heartily, drink *quantum sufficit*, but sleep immoderately.

quem dī dīligunt adolēscēns moritur

~ he whom the gods love dies young.

PLAUTUS *Bacchides* I.817, translating MENANDER *Dis Exapaton* fragment 4 (Sandbach).

Cf. 1546 W. HUGHE *Troubled Man's Medicine* B8v Most happy be they and best belouid of god, that dye whan they be yong.

quem Jupiter vult perdere dēmentat prius (or quem deus perdere vult, prius dēmentat)

~ whom Jupiter (or a god) wishes to destroy, he first makes mad.

J. DUPORT *Homeri Gnomologia* (1660) p. 282. This is based on the scholiast's note on SOPHOCLES *Antigone* 622ff.

quēstiō quid iūris

~ the question is, which part of the law.

This is one of the Latin phrases which Chaucer's Summoner had picked up at the ecclesiastical court without understanding it (General Prologue to the *Canterbury Tales* 640–8).

quicquid agunt hominēs ... nostrī est farrāgo libellī

~ whatever men do is the medley of our little book.

JUVENAL i.85–6.

quicquid dēlīrant rēgēs plectuntur Achīvī

~ whatever madness possesses the chiefs, it is the (ordinary) Achaeans who get hurt.

HORACE *Epistles* I.ii.14. The ordinary soldiers suffer from the folly of their rulers.

quīcunque vult (salvus esse)
∼ whosoever will (be saved).

The beginning of the Athanasian Creed.

quī docet discit
∼ he who teaches learns.

quid sit futūrum crās fuge quaerere
∼ do not ask what is going to happen tomorrow.

HORACE *Odes* I.ix.13. Gather ye rosebuds while ye may, urges the poet.

quid prō quō
∼ something for something, tit for tat.

1591 SHAKESPEARE *1 Henry VI* v.iii.109 I cry you mercy, 'tis but *Quid* for *Quo*.

quid Rōmae faciam?
∼ what can I do at Rome?

JUVENAL iii.41.

quīeta nōn movēre
∼ not to move settled things, i.e. to let sleeping dogs lie.

Based on SALLUST *Catiline* xxi.1.

1771 H. WALPOLE *Letter* 26 Mar. in *Correspondence* (1937) VII.289 My father's maxim, *Quieta non movere*, was very well in those ignorant days.

quiētus
∼ literally, 'rest', i.e. a discharge or acquittance given on payment of sums due, or clearing of accounts; a discharge from office or duty; discharge or release from life.

1540 *Act 32 Hen. VIII* (Pardon), Such issues fines or amerciaments . . . and haue his or their Quietus for the same.

1602 SHAKESPEARE *Hamlet* III.i.75 When he himselfe might his quietus make With a bare bodkin.

quis custōdiet ipsōs custōdēs?
∼ who will guard the guardians themselves?

JUVENAL vi.347–8. Even if you set guards on your wife, she will intrigue with them to gain admission for a lover.

quis fallere possit amantem?
∼ who could deceive a lover?

VIRGIL *Aeneid* iv.296. Dido, with a lover's heightened awareness, has got wind of the fact that Aeneas is planning to abandon her.

quī tacet cōnsentit
~ who keeps silent consents.

quod erat dēmōnstrandum (abbreviated to QED)
~ which was what had to be proved.

This can be added below a mathematical solution.

quod scrīpsī, scrīpsī
~ what I have written, I have written.

JOHN xix.22 in the Vulgate. Pontius Pilate said this in response to the protest at the inscription for the cross of Jesus which read 'Jesus of Nazareth, King of the Jews'.

quod vidē (abbreviated to q.v.)
~ see which thing; a reference, e.g. to another part of a book.

quō iūre?
~ by what right? by what law?

quondam
~ formerly.

'My quondam barber, but "his lordship" now.' DRYDEN

quōrum
~ literally, 'of whom', i.e. a fixed number of members of any body, society etc., whose presence is necessary for the proper or valid transaction of business.

1616 in J. ROW *The historie of the kirk of Scotland 1558–1637* (1842) 81 The Assemblie appoynts twenty Commissioners nominat, whereof six a quorum, to attend the King's Majestie's ansuer.

quōrum pars magna fuī
~ of which things I was a great part.

VIRGIL *Aeneid* ii.6. Aeneas begins his account of the fall of Troy by commenting that he was a leading actor in this dreadful event.

quōs deus vult perdere, prius dēmentat
~ those whom god wishes to destroy he first makes mad.

See QUEM DEUS VULT PERDERE, PRIUS DEMENTAT.

quot homines tot sententiae
~ there are as many opinions as men.

TERENCE *Phormio* II.iv.14.

1539 R. TAVERNER tr. Erasmus's *Proverbes or Adagies* f.xiii Quot homines, tot sententiae. So many heades, so many iudgementes.

quōusque tandem abutēre, Catilīna, patientiā nostrā?
~ how far, Catiline, will you abuse our patience?

CICERO *In Catilinam* I.i.1. Cicero began his first speech against Catiline, whom he accused of conspiring against the Roman republic in 63 BC, with these words.

quō vādis (, domine)?
~ where are you going to (, master)?

PSEUDO-LINUS *Martyrium beati Petri apostoli* 6. The words of St Peter to Jesus. Jesus appeared to Peter as the latter was fleeing Rome to escape Nero's persecution of the Christians. To this question from St Peter, Jesus replied that he was going to Rome to be crucified a second time. St Peter accordingly returned to Rome and was martyred by being crucified upside down.

q.v.
See QUOD VIDE.

rādit usque ad cutem

∼ he shaves right up to the skin, i.e. he drives a hard bargain.

rādīx malōrum est cupiditās

∼ greed is the root of all evils.

1 TIMOTHY vi.10 in the Vulgate. Quoted in Chaucer, Prologue to the *Pardoner's Tale* VI (C) 426.

rāra avis

∼ a 'rare bird' on earth, an exceptional person, a paragon.

JUVENAL vi.165. Better, says the poet, find a slut than a proud paragon among women, who would prove intolerable.

1607 G. WILKINS *Miseries of Inforst Mariage* sig. A3u   And by that, thou hast beene married but three weekes, tho thou shouldst wed a *Cynthia rara avis*, thou wouldest be a man monstrous: A cuckold, a cuckold.

rē

∼ concerning, in the matter of.

rēbus sīc stantibus

∼ things standing thus, i.e. provided that conditions have not changed.

receptō dulce mihi furere est amīcō

∼ it is sweet for me to make merry when I have regained a friend.

HORACE *Odes* II.vii.28. The poet invites his old friend Pompeius to a party to welcome him home.

rēctō

∼ on the right: in printing, the right-hand page of an open book; hence, the front of a leaf as opposed to the back or VERSO.

1824 J. JOHNSON *Typographia* I.217   This . . . volume commences on the recto of the first leaf.

redde legiōnēs!
∾ give me back my legions!

SUETONIUS *Augustus* xxiii.2. After his general Varus lost three legions in a massacre in the Teutoburg Forest in Germany in AD 9, the emperor Augustus was so distressed that he used to beat his head on a door as he shouted out these words.

redivīvus
∾ come back to life.

1675 R. HEAD *Proteus redivivus: or the art of wheedling or insinuation* (title).

redolet lucernā
∾ it smells of the lamp.

See OLET LUCERNA.

reductiō ad absurdum
∾ reduction to the absurd.

First recorded use in English 1741.

1896 G. B. SHAW *Our Theatres in Nineties* (1932) II.170   Madame Sarah Grand's position is a *reductio ad absurdum* of our whole moral system.

referendum
∾ literally, 'something to be referred', i.e. the practice or principle (in early use chiefly associated with the Swiss constitution) of submitting a question at issue to the whole body of voters.

1847 G. GROTE *Letter* 25 Sept. in *Seven Letters concerning Politics Switzerland* (1847) iv.81   The clergy made efficient use of their influence over the popular *referendum*.

1977 *Times* 17 Mar. 19/3   They did not tell us at the time of the referendum that Brussels was to reform the English language.

rēgīna
∾ a queen.

Used (with a capital R) to designate the prosecution in criminal proceedings during the reign of a queen, as in law reports, e.g. '*Regina* v. *Kellett*'. Cf. REX.

rēligiō lāicī
∾ the religion of a layman. The title of a poem written in 1682

by Dryden in which he explains his Anglican religious faith.
In 1686 he became a Roman Catholic.

rēligiō locī
~ the religious spirit of the place.

VIRGIL viii.349. As Evander takes Aeneas on a tour of the future site of
Rome, the poet says that even then what was to be the Capitol had a god-
haunted feel.

rem acū tetigistī
~ literally, 'you have touched the thing with a needle', i.e. you
have hit the nail on the head.

PLAUTUS *Rudens* V.ii.19.

requiēscat in pāce (abbreviated to RIP)
~ may he/she rest in peace; a wish for the repose of the dead.

rēs angusta domī
~ straitened circumstances at home.

JUVENAL iii.165. Such conditions make it hard for someone to rise in the
world.

rēs in cardine est
~ the matter is on a hinge, i.e. it's a critical juncture in a situation.

rēs ipsa loquitur
~ literally, 'the thing itself speaks', i.e. the matter speaks for
itself.

Based on CICERO *Pro Milone* 53.

respice fīnem
~ look to the end.

Jocularly perverted into *respice funem*, beware the hangman's rope (*finem* =
end, *funem* = rope).

resurgam
~ I shall rise again.

retrō mē, satanā,
~ get thee behind me, Satan.

MATTHEW xvi.23, MARK viii.33, LUKE iv.8. (in Vulgate VADE RETRO ME,
SATANA) Stop trying to tempt me.

rēx

~ a king.

Used (with a capital R) to designate the prosecution in criminal proceedings during the reign of a king, e.g. *Rex* v. *Hall*. Cf. REGINA.

rīdendō dīcere vērum

~ to tell the truth with laughter.

Based on HORACE *Satires* I.i.24–5. This could be said to be the aim of satire. Cf. John Marston (1576–1634): 'In serious jest, and jesting seriousness, I strive to scourge polluting beastliness.'

rīdē sī sapis

~ laugh if you are wise.

MARTIAL II.xli.1.

RIP *See* REQUIESCAT IN PACE.

rīsum teneātis, amīcī?

~ can you hold back your laughter, friends?

HORACE *Ars Poetica* 5.

Rōma locūta est; causa fīnīta est

~ Rome (i.e. the Pope) has spoken; the case is concluded.

ST AUGUSTINE *Sermons* I.

ruat coelum

~ though the heaven fall.

See FIAT IUSTITIA ET RUANT COELI.

rūs in urbe

~ literally, 'the country in the city'.

MARTIAL XII.lvii.21.

1759 T. GRAY *Letter* 24 July (1827) II.40   I am now settled in my new territories commanding Bedford gardens, and all the fields as far as Highgate and Hampstead . . .; so *rus-in-urbe-ish*, that I believe I shall stay here.

saeva indignātiō *See* UBI SAEVA INDIGNATIO . . .

sal Atticum
    ~ 'Attic salt', i.e. wit (which, like salt, gives life or character to a thing) appropriate to the classical Athenians (whose city was in Attica); thus, refined, delicate, poignant wit.

    Cf. 1760 L. STERNE *Tristram Shandy* V.iii Triumph swam in my father's eyes, at the repartee: the Attic salt brought water into them.

salūs populī suprēma lēx estō
    ~ let the good of the people be the chief law.

    CICERO *De Legibus* III.viii.8.

salvā vēritāte
    ~ saving the truth, i.e. without infringement of truth.

salvē (plural salvēte)
    ~ hail!

    A Roman greeting.

    1583 R. GREENE *Mamillia* in *Works*, II.22 After he had curteously giuen her the *Salve*.

sal volātile
    ~ ammonium carbonate, especially an aromatic solution of this used as a restorative in fainting fits.

    1654 EDMUND GAYTON *Pleasant Notes upon Don Quixot* IV.v.197 'Tis that fire, that *sal volatile* which makes them of so strange agility.

sāncta simplicitās
    ~ holy simplicity, an expression of astonishment at another's naïvety.

Said to have been the dying words of John Huss (1373–1415), Bohemian religious reformer and martyr, provoked by the sight of a simple peasant adding wood to the fire about his stake.

First recorded use in English 1847.

1889 G. B. SHAW in *Star* 13 July 4/4 She ... thinks it would be too much to ask the public to listen to two sonatas.*Sancta simplicitas!* too much!

sānctum sānctōrum

∼ the holy of holies, i.e. the Jewish temple and tabernacle; hence used of any supremely holy location.

First recorded use in English 1400.

?1493 *St. Katherine* (W. de W.) b iij a/1 (Stanf.) That holy place that is called Sancta sanctorum.

sapere audē

∼ dare to be wise.

HORACE *Epistles* I.ii.40. The poet exhorts Lollius Maximus not to delay but to reform his way of life now.

sartor resartus

∼ the tailor retailored.

The title of a book by Thomas Carlyle (1795–1881) which makes use of the metaphor of clothing to expound a philosophy of life.

satis

∼ enough.

One use of this word is in the marking of essays, where it signifies that the quality is adequate but no more.

satis ēloquentiae, sapientiae parum

∼ plenty of eloquence, (but) too little wisdom.

Sāturnālia

∼ in Roman times the festival of Saturn, held in the middle of December and observed as a time of general merrymaking, extending even to the slaves; hence a period of unrestrained licence and revelry.

1591 L. LLOYD *Trpl. Triumphes* B3 Imitating the orders and maners in the feast Saturnalia.

1818 BYRON *Childe Harold* IV.xcvii But France got drunk with blood to vomit crime, And fatal have her Saturnalia been, To Freedom's cause.

sc. *See* SCILICET.

scāla Caelī

~ the ladder of heaven: the name of a church in the Tre Fontane, outside Rome, in which St Bernard is related to have had a vision of souls for whom he was saying Mass ascending by a ladder into heaven, and to which an indulgence was attached; hence, applied to chapels or altars in England and the masses said there to which the same indulgence was attached; also a ladder leading from earth to heaven; a means of attaining heaven or heavenly bliss.

First recorded use in English 1380.

1626 F. BACON *New Atlantis* 15 The Magnificent Temple, . . . the seuerall Degrees of Ascent, wherby Men did climb vp to the same, as if it had bin a Scala Caeli.

scāla nātūrae

~ literally, 'ladder of nature', the chain of being.

Cf. 1859 C. DARWIN *Origin of Species* v.149 Beings low in the scale of nature are more variable than those which are higher.

1983 E. C. MINKOFF *Evolutionary Biology* iii.50/2 Buffon's criticisms of Linnaeus were several. He objected especially to any arbitrary subdivision of nature, for he believed that the *scala naturae* was a continuum.

scandalum magnātum

~ 'scandal of magnates', the utterance or publication of any malicious report against any person holding a position of dignity.

The term was suggested by the wording of the statute 2 Ric. II stat. 1c.5, which provides penalties for the offence.

1607 T. MIDDLETON *The Phoenix* F j b A Writ of Delay, Longsword. *Scandala Magnatum*, Backesword.

schola cantōrum

~ school of singers: the choir-school attached to a cathedral or monastery (originally the Papal Choir at Rome, established by Gregory the Great (*c.* 540–604); also used of various groups of singers.

1782 C. BURNEY *General History of Music* II.i.16 Fleury, in his *Hist. Eccl* . . . gives a circumstantial account of the *Scola Cantorum*, instituted by St. Gregory.

scīlicet (abbreviated to **scil.** or **sc.**)
~ that is to say, namely.

First recorded use in English 1387.

1547 J. HOOPER *A declaracion of Christe and of his offyce* xii. L vijb God sentithe
an other mystres to scole man, scilicet aduersitie.

Scotōrum perfervida ingenia *See* PERFERVIDUM INGENIUM
SCOTORUM.

scrīpsit
~ he/she wrote (it).

Used with the author's name.

sculpsit
~ he/she sculptured or engraved (it).

Used with the sculptor's or engraver's name.

sed haec hāctenus
~ but enough of this—now we can move on to something else.

semel īnsānīvimus omnēs
~ we have all played the fool once.

J. B. MANTUANUS *Eclogues* i.217.

semper eadem
~ always the same.

The motto of Queen Elizabeth I.

semper fidēlis
~ always faithful.

Senatus Populusque Romanus (abbreviated to **SPQR**)
~ the Senate (the governing body of Rome) and the Roman
People.

On every drain cover and on every bus in Rome there is this inscription.

senex bis puer
~ the old man is twice a child, i.e. in his dotage the old man
becomes a child again in his helplessness and lack of clear
judgement.

sēnsū lātō

~ in the broad sense (the opposite of the next entry).

1942 W. B. TURNBULL in *Bot. Rev.* VIII.656 (heading) Algae (sensu lato).

sēnsū strictō

~ literally, 'in the restricted meaning', i.e. strictly speaking, in the narrow sense of a term.

1941 J. S. HUXLEY *Uniqueness of Man* xi.240 Human biology is but an extension of biology *sensu stricto*.

seq. (abbreviation of sequēns)

~ following.

The plural form is *seqq.*, abbreviating *sequentēs*; it is often preceded by *et* (= and).

1726 J. KER *Mem.* i. (1727) Index Scotland, a View of their Affairs. 113, 131, & *seq.*

sērō venientibus ossa

~ the bones to the late-comers.

if you arrive late, you will find that all the meat has been eaten.

sesquipedālia verba

~ words a foot and a half long.

HORACE *Ars Poetica* 97. The poet is arguing for the use of appropriate diction in comedy and tragedy but here makes the point that sometimes a character in tragedy can abandon bombastic language (the *sesquipedalia verba*) and touch the spectator's heart by simple directness.

sīc

~ literally, 'thus'. Used as a parenthetical insertion in printing quotations or reported utterances to call attention to something anomalous or erroneous in the original, or to guard against the supposition of misquotation, e.g. in 'As for what Miss Lynch calls "his really serious affair with Harriet" (I feel this deserves a *sic*), it is purely theatrical.' (*Scrutiny*, Sept. 1937, 131)

sīc erat in fātīs

~ so it was fated.

OVID *Fasti* i.481. Evander is reassured by his mother that his banishment from Arcadia is due to no fault on his part. It was fated.

sīc ītur ad astra
∼ thus one may go to the stars (i.e. to immortal fame).

VIRGIL *Aeneid* ix.641. Aeneas's young son Ascanius kills the Italian Remulus by transfixing his temples with an arrow. The god Apollo looks down from a cloud and addresses the youthful hero with these words.

sīc passim
∼ thus everywhere.

Used e.g. in instructions to typesetters, such as 'Put the title of the play *King Lear* into italics, and *sic passim* (i.e. do this throughout the manuscript)'.

sīc semper tyrannīs
∼ thus ever to tyrants.

The motto of the State of Virginia; also said to have been shouted by John Wilkes Booth after he had assassinated Abraham Lincoln in 1865.

sīc trānsit glōria mundī
∼ thus passes away the glory of the world.

Possibly an adaptation of a passage of Thomas à Kempis, meaning 'Oh how quickly the world's glory passes away' (*Of the Imitation of Christ*, I.iii.6). The Latin words are spoken during the coronation of a new Pope while flax is burned to represent the transitoriness of earthly glory. They were used at the coronation of Alexander V at Pisa on 7 July 1409, but are earlier in origin.

1601 B. JONSON *Every Man in his Humour* v.i. sig. Mv See, see, how our Poets glory shines brighter and brighter, still, still it increaseth, oh now its at the highest, and now it declines as fast: you may see gallants, *sic transit gloria mundi*.

sī dīs placet
∼ if it pleases the gods.

silent lēgēs inter arma
∼ the laws are silent amid arms.

CICERO *Pro Milone* iv.11. Cicero argues that, when one's life is threatened by violent plots and the laws have been reduced to silence, one has the right of self-defence in any way possible.

similia similibus cūrantur
∼ like things are cured by like things.

The basic principle of homeopathy, a system of medical practice founded by Samuel Hahnemann of Leipzig about 1796, according to which diseases are treated by the administration (usually in very small does) of drugs which would produce in a healthy person symptoms closely related to those of the disease being treated.

sī monumentum requīris, circumspice
~ if you seek (his) monument, look about you.

The inscription on the tomb of Sir Christopher Wren (1632–1723) in St Paul's Cathedral, London, which he built. The words are also the motto of the State of Michigan.

simplex munditiīs
~ simple in your adornments, i.e. unostentatiously beautiful, elegantly simple.

HORACE *Odes* I.v.5. Milton translates this, hardly satisfactorily, as 'plain in your neatness'. Horace is writing of Pyrrha, a former girlfriend. He wonders who's kissing her now.

sine diē
~ literally, 'without a day' i.e. indefinitely, until an unspecified date.

1631 in THOMAS BIRCH *The court and times of Charles the first* (1848) II.125 My Lord of Salisbury's cause is put off *sine die*.

sine īrā et studiō
~ without either anger or partiality.

TACITUS *Annals* I.i. The historian, as he embarks on his devastating account of the early Roman empire, claims, many feel disingenuously, that he is free of these emotions.

sine quā nōn
~ literally, 'without which not', i.e. somebody or something indispensable.

First recorded use in English 1602.

1814 *Amer. St. Papers, For. Relat.* (1832) III.709 It was a *sine qua non* that the Indians should be included in the pacification.

sint Maecēnātēs, nōn deerunt, Flacce, Marōnes
~ if you have (patrons like) Maecenas, Flaccus, you won't miss out on Virgils.

MARTIAL VIII.lv.5. The point is that if you have a good patron (as Maecenas had proved to the poets of the Augustan era), you will blossom as a poet. A Virgil needs a Maecenas if he is to produce his best work.

sī parva licet compōnere magnīs
~ if I am allowed to compare small things to great.

VIRGIL *Georgics* iv.176. See PARVA COMPONERE MAGNIS. And cf. *sī compōnere magnīs parva mihī fās est* (if it is right for me to compare small things to great), Ovid's imitation of (and thus tribute to) Virgil (*Metamorphoses* v.416–17).

siste, viātor
~ stop, traveller.

An inscription on Roman tombstones.

sit nōn doctissima coniūnx
~ may my wife not be extremely learned.

situs inversus
~ inverted disposition (of the internal organs), i.e. the condition in which the organs of the body are transposed through the sagittal plane (so that the heart lies on the right side, etc.).

sī vīs amārī, amā
~ if you wish to be loved, love!

SENECA *Epistles* ix.4.

si vīs pācem, parā bellum
~ if you want peace, be ready for war.

Based on VEGETIUS *Epitome rei militaris* iii prologue.

sōlitūdinem faciunt, pācem appellant
~ they make a desert (and) call it peace.

TACITUS *Agricola* xxx. The Scottish leader Calgacus rouses his followers with this scathing denunciation of the *pax Romana* (*See under* PAX).

solvitur ambulandō
~ literally, 'it [the problem] is solved by walking'.

Used of an appeal to practical experience for the solution of a problem or proof of a statement. First recorded use in English 1852.

1863 J. CONINGTON *Horace's Odes* p. xxv How easily the '*solvitur ambulando*' of an artist like Mr. Tennyson may disturb a whole chain of ingenious reasoning on the possibilities of things.

solventur rīsū tabulae: tū missus abībis

~ the indictment will dissolve in laughter, and you'll go scot free (*translation by Niall Rudd*).

HORACE *Satires* II.i.86. If you write good satire against a public menace and lead a blameless life yourself, you'll get away with it.

spectātum veniunt, veniunt spectentur ut ipsae

~ they come to see, they come to be seen themselves.

OVID *Ars Amatoria* i.99. The poet stresses the advantages of the theatre, to which available women flock, as a splendid pick-up location. Dryden memorably translates this and the following line: 'To see, and to be seen, in Heaps they run; Some to undo, and some to be undone.'

spērō meliōra

~ I hope for better things.

splendidē mendāx

~ splendidly false, nobly untruthful.

HORACE *Odes* III.xi.35. Hypermnestra was nobly loyal to her husband when she saved his life by betraying her father's plan to kill him.

SPQR

See SENATUS POPULUSQUE ROMANUS.

sprētaeque iniūria fōrmae

~ and the insult to beauty slighted.

VIRGIL *Aeneid* i.27. One reason for Juno's hatred of the Trojans is that the Trojan prince Paris did not give her the prize in a beauty competition with Venus (who won) and Minerva.

Stābat Māter (dolōrōsa)

~ stood the mother (full of grief).

A sequence composed by Jacobus de Benedictis in the thirteenth century, in commemoration of the sorrows of the Virgin Mary; also a musical setting of this sequence.

stāre dēcīsīs

~ literally, 'to stand by things decided', i.e. the legal principle of determining points in litigation according to precedent.

1782 F. BULLER in E. H. East *Reports of cases argued and determined in the court of king's bench* (1801) I.495 The rule *stare decisis* is one of the most sacred in the law.

stat magnī nōminis umbrā

~ he stands in the shadow of a great name.

See MAGNI NOMINIS UMBRA.

status quō

~ literally, 'the state in which', i.e. the existing state of affairs.

1833 *Edinburgh Review* LVI.436 The *status quo* was to be maintained in Luxemburg during negotiations respecting that duchy.

status quō ante (bellum)

~ the state of affairs existing before (the war).

stet

~ let it stand: a direction in the margin of a proof or manuscript that matter which has been altered or struck out is to remain uncorrected.

1755 J. SMITH *Printer's Grammar* xi.277 Where words are struck out that are afterwards again approved of, they mark dots under such words, and write in the Margin, *Stet.*

stet fortūna domūs

~ may the fortune of the house last long.

A motto (e.g. of Harrow School), based on VIRGIL *Georgics* iv.209. Virgil's words are used of a flourishing community of bees.

stultōrum calamī carbōnēs, moenia chartae

~ chalk is the pen for fools and walls their paper.

An attack on graffiti.

stupor mundī

~ the marvel of the world: an object of admiring bewilderment and wonder.

The phrase was originally used by the thirteenth-century historian Matthew Paris to describe Emperor Frederick II of Germany.

1879 *Encyclopaedia Britannica* IX.732/2 The general contemporary opinion regarding Frederick II is expressed in the words *stupor mundi* ... wonder and perplexity are the predominant sentiments which ... [the contemplation of his career] even yet awakens.

sua cuique voluptās

~ everyone has his own pleasures.

STATIUS *Silvae* II.ii.73. Cf. the English proverb 'every man to his taste' and the French equivalent 'chacun à son goût'.

suāviter in modō, fortiter in rē

~ gentle in manner, resolute in deed.

sub dīō

~ under the open sky, in the open air.

1611 T. CORYAT *Crudities* 28 He walked not *sub dio*, that is, vnder the open aire as the rest did.

sub iūdice

~ literally, 'under a judge', i.e. under the consideration of a judge or court; undecided, not yet settled, still under consideration.

1613 J. CHAMBERLAIN in *Court and times of James the first* (1848) I.279 Lord Hay is like ... to be made an earl, but whether English or Scottish is yet *sub judice*.

sub līte

~ in dispute.

sub poenā

~ literally, 'under the penalty of'.

The origin of the English word *subpoena*, a writ issued by chancery commanding the presence of a defendant to answer the matter alleged against him.

sub rosā

~ literally, 'under the rose', in secret, secretly.

1654 EDMUND GAYTON *Pleasant Notes upon Don Quixot* III.v.93 What ever thou and the foule pusse did doe (*sub Rosa* as they say).

sub speciē aeternitātis

~ 'under the aspect of eternity', i.e. viewed in relation to the eternal; in a universal perspective.

1896 W. CALDWELL *Schopenhauer's System* v.268 Art enables us somehow to see things *sub specie aeternitatis*.

suggestiō falsī

~ suggestion of what is false, i.e. a misrepresentation of the truth whereby something incorrect is implied to be true; an indirect lie.

Cf. SUPPRESSIO VERI, SUGGESTIO FALSI.

1815 H. MADDOCK *Principles and Practice of Chancery* I.208 Whenever *Suppressio veri* or *Suggestio falsi* occur ... they afford a sufficient ground for setting aside any Release or Conveyance.

suī generis

~ literally, 'of his/her/its particular kind', i.e. forming a kind by itself.

1787 M. CUTLER in *Life*, etc. (1888) I.268 The Doctor ... thinks it must be a *sui generis* of that class of animals.

suī iūris

~ literally, 'of one's own right', i.e. of full age and capacity.

1675 MARQUIS OF WORCESTER in *Essex Papers* 38 Shee is of an age not only of consent and dissent but to be sui iuris.

summā cum laude

~ with highest praise.

The superlative of MAGNA CUM LAUDE.

summum bonum

~ the highest good, i.e. the chief or supreme good. An ethical term and often in trivial or jocular use.

1563 T. GALE *Certaine workes of chirurgerie* II As one myght thynke hymselfe ryght happye, though he neuer dyd attayne to Aristoteles *summum bonum*, or Plato his idea.

sunt aliquid Mānēs: lētum nōn omnia fīnit

~ the spirits of the dead do have an existence: death does not finish everything.

PROPERTIUS IV.vii.1. The ghost of the poet's mistress has appeared to him.

sunt lacrimae rērum

~ there are tears over things.

See LACRIMAE RERUM.

suppressiō vērī, suggestiō falsī

~ suppression of the true (is) suggestion of the false. *See* SUGGESTIO FALSI.

suprā

~ above, i.e. previously, before (in a book or writing). Also *vidē suprā* see above.

First recorded use in English 1440.

1861 FRED. A. PALEY *The tragedies of Aeschylus* (edn.2) *Supplices* 953 (note) On the metre of this verse see supra 7.

173

sūrsum corda

∿ lift up your hearts.

Part of the Latin Eucharist.

sūs Minervam

∿ literally, 'a pig (teaches) Minerva (the goddess of wisdom)', i.e. teach one's grandmother to suck eggs (i.e. to teach someone something which they know far more about than their teacher).

CICERO *Academica* I.xviii.8 & *Ad Familiares* IX.xviii.4. This proverb, of Greek origin, is based on a story which has been lost, perhaps about a pig challenging Minerva to a music competition.

sūtor nē suprā crepidam iūdicāret

∿ let not the cobbler criticize (a work of art) above the sandal.

See NE SUTOR ULTRA CREPIDAM.

tābula rāsa

~ a smooth or blank tablet, i.e. a tablet from which the writing has been erased, and which is therefore ready to be written upon again.

Usually used figuratively. First recorded use in English 1535.

1875 B. JOWETT *Plato* (edn. 2) III.73 The artist will do nothing until he has made a tabula rasa.

tacent, satis laudant

~ their silence is praise enough.

TERENCE *Eunuchus* III.ii.23. One character in Plautus' play assumes that another's silence betokens high approval.

tacet

~ there is silence.

A direction in music that the voice or instrument is to be silent for a time.

taedium vītae

~ weariness of life; extreme ennui or inertia, sometimes regarded as a pathological state.

First recorded use in English 1618.

1891 O. WILDE *Picture of Dorian Gray* xi.216 That ennui, that terrible *taedium vitae*, that comes on those to whom life denies nothing.

tantae mōlis erat Rōmānam condere gentem

~ a task of such effort was it to found the Roman race.

VIRGIL *Aeneid* i.33. The effort involved in founding Rome is one of the great themes of the *Aeneid*.

tantaene animīs caelestibus īrae?

~ can there be such anger in the spirits of the gods?

VIRGIL *Aeneid* i.11. Almost until the end of the *Aeneid*, the powerful goddess Juno harries the Trojans with unremitting rage. With this question, which Virgil asks at the end of the poem's first paragraph, he raises one of the work's most tragic themes.

tantum rēligiō potuit suādēre malōrum

~ religion has been able to lead men to commit so many evils.

LUCRETIUS *De Rerum Natura* i.101. The philosophical poet deplores the crimes committed owing to religious belief.

tempora (originally omnia) mūtantur, nōs et mūtāmur in illīs

~ times change and we change with them.

A saying (in the form with *omnia*) ascribed to the emperor Lothair I.

1577 W. HARRISON *Description Britayne* III.iii.99 in R. Holinshed *Chronicles* I
Oft in one age, diuers iudgementes doe passe upon one maner of casse,
wherby the saying of the poet *Tempora mutantur, & nos mutamur in illis.*

tempus, edāx rērum

~ time, consumer of things.

OVID *Metamorphoses* xv.234. Everything wastes away.

tempus fugit

~ time flies.

tenēre lupum auribus

~ to hold a wolf by the ears.

See LUPUM AURIBUS TENERE.

terminus ad quem

~ literally, 'term to which', i.e. the finishing time of something.

1555 T. CRANMER *Lord's Supper* (Parker Soc.) 272 In nutrition *terminus a quo*
[*see next entry*] is the hunger and thirst of the man; and *terminus ad quem* is
the feeding and satisfying of his hunger and thirst.

terminus ā quō

~ literally, 'end from which', i.e. the starting-point of something.

See quotation in previous entry.

terra firma

~ literally, 'firm land', i.e. the land as distinguished from the sea.

1693 RAY *Disc.* i.iii.24 The whole *terra firma*, or dry Land.

terra incognita

∼ unknown land, i.e. an unknown or unexplored region.

1616 CAPT. SMITH *Description New England* 6 The Spaniards know . . . not so much as the true circumference of *Terra Incognita*, whose large dominions may equalize the greatnesse and goodnes of America.

tertius gaudēns

∼ literally, 'a third (party) rejoicing', i.e. a third party that benefits by the conflict or estrangement of two others.

1892 tr. Bismarck in *Ann. Reg. 1891* 284 I should like to interfere in such cases, like a parish beadle bringing peace, and prove that the *tertius gaudens* is the worst enemy.

theātrum mundī

∼ the theatre of the world: the theatre thought of as a presentation of all aspects of human life.

1566 J. ALDAY tr. P. Boaistuau (title) Theatrum Mundi, the Theatre or rule of the world, wherein may be sene the running race and course of everye mans life, as touching miserie and felicity, wherein is contained wonderfull examples, learned devices, to the overthrow of vice, and exalting of vertue.

timeō Danaōs et dōna ferentēs

∼ I fear the Greeks even when they bring gifts.

VIRGIL *Aeneid* ii.49. Laocoon, the Trojan priest of Neptune, strongly urges his countrymen not to accept the apparent gift of the Trojan horse from the Greeks. This will, of course, effect their downfall. These words have now become a semi-proverbial expression with the slightly different meaning of 'I fear the Greeks *especially* when they bring gifts'.

tolle lege, tolle lege

∼ take up (the book) and read, take up (the book) and read.

ST AUGUSTINE *Confessions* VIII.xii.29. The saint recalls how a boy or a girl repeatedly chanting these words from a neighbouring house led him to take up the Bible again.

totidem verbīs

∼ in so many words.

1659 B. HARDY *First Ep. John* vi.101 We do not read (*totidem verbis*) in the Scripture that the Apostle Baptized Infants, yet it is very probable.

trahit sua quemque voluptās

∼ each man's fancy lures him.

VIRGIL *Eclogues* ii.65. The shepherd Corydon is obsessed by his master's handsome favourite Alexis.

trāicit et fātī lītora magnus amor

~ a great love can cross the bounds even of fate.

PROPERTIUS I.xix.12. Love can transcend even death—one of the supreme lines of love poetry.

trīstis eris sī sōlus eris

~ you will be sad if you are on your own.

OVID *Remedia Amoris* 583.

Trōia fuit

~ Troy has been (i.e. exists no longer).

PROPERTIUS II.viii.10. Everything changes. Troy once stood high, but now no longer.

tū nē cēde malīs sed contrā audentior ītō

~ do not you yield to misfortunes but advance the more boldly against them.

VIRGIL *Aeneid* vi.95. Apollo's priestess at Cumae in south Italy utters a terrifying prediction of his future to Aeneas but tells him to bear up.

tū quoque

~ you too, you're another, i.e. an argument which consists in retorting a charge upon one's accusers.

First recorded use in English 1614.

1874 J. O. DYKES *Relations Kingd. to World* ii.107 The tu quoque rejoinder, 'Physician heal thyself', is in its place here.

U

ubi bene, ibi patria
~ where things go well, there is one's fatherland.

Based on CICERO *Tusculan Disputations* V.xxxvii.108.

ubi mel, ibi apēs
~ where there is honey there are bees.

ubi saeva indignātiō ulterius cor lacerāre nequit
~ where fierce indignation can tear his heart no longer.

Part of the epitaph on the acid satirist Jonathan Swift (1667–1745).

ubi sōlitūdinem faciunt pācem appellant
~ where they make a desert they call it peace.

See SOLITUDINEM FACIUNT, PACEM APPELLANT.

ubi sunt?
~ literally, 'where are?'

An interrogatory phrase taken from the opening words or the refrain of certain medieval Latin works, used chiefly to designate a mood or theme in literature of lament for the mutability of things.

1914 B. C. WILLIAMS *Gnomic Poetry in Anglo-Saxon* 45 The *ubi sunt* motivation is an old one, perhaps of equal age with riddle, charm, and spell.

ultima ratiō
~ final sanction.

1848 J. S. MILL *Political Economy* I.ii.ix.375 The Irish cottier . . . protects himself by the *ultima ratio* of a defensive civil war.

ultima Thūlē
~ farthest Thule (a land six days' sail north of Britain, supposed in antiquity to be the most northerly region in the world; variously conjectured to be the Shetland Islands,

Iceland, or points in Denmark or Norway); thus, the extreme limit of travel or discovery; the highest or uttermost point attained or attainable.

1771 T. SMOLLETT *Humphry Clinker* 3 Sept. I am now little short of the *Ultima Thule*, if this appellation properly belongs to the Orkneys or Hebrides.

1828 *Lights & Shades* II.136 The caricature of a fop, the *ultima Thule* of extravagant frippery.

ultimus Rōmānōrum
~ the last of the Romans.

The Latin version of the Greek of PLUTARCH *Brutus* 84, Brutus' tribute to the dead Cassius, who with him had been one of the leading assassins of Julius Caesar. Shakespeare's memorable line in *Julius Caesar* (V.iii.99) runs 'The last of all the Romans, fare thee well!'

ultrā vīrēs
~ beyond the powers or legal authority (of a person).

1793 [EARL DUNDONALD] *Descr. Estate Culross* 59 This had proved, and must always prove, *ultra vires* for any one individual.

ūna salūs victīs nūllam spērāre salūtem
~ the one safety for the defeated is to have no hope of safety.

VIRGIL *Aeneid* ii.354. Aeneas thus eggs on the Trojans to frenzied slaughter on the night of the fall of Troy when he thinks that they are doomed.

ūnō saltū duōs aprōs capere
~ literally, 'to take two boars in one valley', i.e. to kill two birds with one stone.

PLAUTUS *Casina* II.viii.4.

urbem latericiam invēnit, marmoream relīquit
~ he (the Roman emperor Augustus) found the city (of Rome) brick (and) left it marble.

SUETONIUS *Augustus* 28.

urbī et ōrbī
~ to the city (of Rome) and the world.

Used in official announcements such as papal bulls.

1867 *Chambers's Encyclopaedia* IX.671/2 *Urbi et Orbi* ... a form used in the publication of papal bullls, for the purpose of signifying their formal promulgation to the entire Catholic world, as well as to the city of Rome.

urbs antīqua ruit, multōs domināta per annōs

~ there falls an ancient city which had held sway for many years.

VIRGIL *Aeneid* ii.363. The city of Troy is referred to here: Aeneas is describing its sack by the Greeks.

usque ad nauseam

~ right up to sickness.

See AD NAUSEAM.

ūtī forō

~ to play the market.

TERENCE *Phormio* 79.

utinam ūnam cervīcem habēret!

~ if only (the Roman crowd) had one neck!

SUETONIUS *Caligula* xxx.2. This was reportedly the emperor Caligula's exclamation at the games when the crowd cheered the team which he opposed.

ut pictūra poēsis

~ a poem is like a picture.

HORACE *Ars Poetica* 361. Viewing conditions and quality make a basic difference.

uti possidētis

~ literally, 'as you possess', in the Roman law an interdict whereby the colourable possession of real property by a *bona fide* possessor was continued until the rights of parties were finally determined.

First recorded use in English 1681.

1823 BYRON *Don Juan* X.xlv.75 A sort of treaty or negotiation, Between the British cabinet and Russian, . . . Something about the Baltic's navigation, Hides, train-oil, tallow, and the rights of Thetis, Which Britons deem their 'uti possidetis'.

ut suprā (abbreviated to ut sup.)

~ as above, i.e. as before (in a book or writing).

1450 in J. STAINER *Early Bodleian Music Sacred & Secular Songs* (1901) I no. lxii, Chorus ut supra What tydynges.

V

vāde in pāce
~ go in peace.

vāde mēcum
~ literally, 'go with me', i.e. a book or manual suitable for carrying about with one for ready reference; a handbook or guidebook.

First recorded use in English 1629.

1731 H. FIELDING *Grub-Street Opera Introduction* It is a sort of family Opera. The husband's vade-mecum; and is very necessary for all married men to have in their houses.

vāde retrō mē, satanā
See RETRO ME, SATANA.

vae victīs
~ woe to the conquered.

LIVY V.xlviii.9. In about 387 BC the Romans were besieged by the Gauls on the Capitol and decided to buy them off with 1,000 pounds' weight in gold. The Gauls, however, used especially heavy weights in order to cheat the Romans. When they complained, Brennus, the barbarian leader, threw his sword into the scale making it even heavier, and exclaimed, 'Vae victis.' But at this moment a Roman army appeared on the scene and wiped out the Gauls' forces.

valē
~ farewell.

1550 M. COVERDALE tr. Wermullerus's *Treatise on Death* Preface iiijb Vale, Loue God, leue vanitye, and lyue in Chryst.

variōrum
~ literally, 'of various persons', i.e. an edition, especially of

the complete works of a classical author, containing the notes of various commentators or editiors.

varium et mūtābile semper fēmina
∼ a woman is an unstable creature, forever changing.

VIRGIL *Aeneid* iv.569. Mercury warns Aeneas in a dream that if he doesn't set off from Africa at once, the changeable Dido will destroy his fleet. This is untrue, and the assessment of Dido is shockingly unjust.

Cf. the Duke of Montua's famous song *La donn' è mobile* (Fickle is woman fair) from the opera *Rigoletto* by Guiseppe Verdi and F. M. Piave (1851).

vendidit hic aurō patriam
∼ this man has sold his fatherland for gold.

VIRGIL *Aeneid* vi.621. Such a man is an inhabitant of Tartarus, the place for the worst sinners, in the underworld.

venī Creātor Spīritus
∼ come, Creator Spirit.

The beginning of an early Latin hymn.

venientī occurrite morbō
∼ run to meet disease as it comes.

PERSIUS iii.63. Don't wait for the sickness to develop; nip it in the bud.

vēnī, vīdī, vīcī
∼ I came, I saw, I conquered.

SUETONIUS *Caesar* xxxvii.2. The famously crisp words of Caesar on his victory over Pharnaces, King of Pontus, in 47 BC.

vēra incessū patuit dea
∼ she was revealed as a true goddess by the way she walked.

VIRGIL *Aeneid* i.405. Aeneas's mother Venus has appeared to him disguised as a huntress, but as she leaves him, she enables him to recognize her.

verbum sat sapientī (abbreviated to **verbum sap.** or **verb. sap.**)
∼ a word is sufficient to a wise person.

An expression used in place of making a full statement or explanation, implying that an intelligent person may easily understand what is left unsaid, or understand the reasons for reticence. A combination of Plautus and Terence.

First recorded use in English 1602.

1862 W. COLLINS *No Name* III.12 I say no more. *Verbum sap.*

vēritās nunquam perit
~ truth never dies.

SENECA *Troades* 614.

vēritās odium parit
~ truth begets hatred.

TERENCE *Andria* I.i.68.

Vergilium vīdī tantum
~ Virgil I only saw.

OVID *Tristia* IV.x.51. Ovid is here writing of his personal knowledge of the great Augustan poets.

versō
~ literally, 'turned', i.e. the back of a leaf in a manuscript or printed book. The left-hand page of a book is the *verso* of that leaf, and faces the RECTO of the next.

versus (abbreviated to ver., vs., or v.)
~ against.

1447-8 J. SHILLINGFORD *Letters and Papers* (Camden) 53 Also the jugement by twene . . . John Husset *versus* John Notte.

1822 SCOTT *Peveril* Prefatory Epistle She may sue me for damages, as in the case Dido *versus* Virgil.

Via Crucis
~ 'the Way of the Cross' (referring to the journey of Jesus as he carried his cross to Golgotha where he was to be crucified).

Thus, an extremely painful experience that has to be borne with fortitude.

Via Dolōrōsa
~ the Way of Sorrow, the route in Jerusalem that Christ is believed to have followed from Pilate's judgement hall to Golgotha; an extremely painful experience that has to be borne with fortitude.

1878 R. L. STEVENSON *Inland Voyage* 186 Fitly enough may the potentate bestride his charger, like a centurion in an old German print of the *Via Dolorosa* . . .

1984 *Observer* 25 Nov. 9/2 Whatever might have happened to other 'wets' on their *via dolorosa* between 1979 and 1983, it was . . . hardly on the cards that Mrs Thatcher would simply drop Peter Walker.

Via Lactea

∼ the Milky Way (galaxy).

It is called 'milky' because the eye sees it as a stream of milky light. Milton wrote (*Paradise Lost* vii.577–81):

A broad and ample road, whose dust is gold
And pavement stars, as stars to thee appear,
Seen in the galaxy—that Milky Way,
Which, nightly, as a circling zone, thou seest
Powdered with stars.

via media

∼ a middle way.

1834 J. H. NEWMAN *Via Media* (Tracts for the Times no. 38) sig. A3v The glory of the English Church is that it has taken the Via Media . . . It lies *between* the (so called) Reformers and the Romanists.

vice versā

∼ literally, 'things having been reversed', i.e. with a reversal or transposition of the main items in the statement just made; conversely.

1601 A. COPLEY *Answere to a Letter of a Jesuited Gentleman* 23 They are like to bee put to such a penance and the Arch-Priests *vice-versa* to be suspended and attained as Schismaticall.

victor lūdōrum

∼ victor of the games, i.e. the overall champion in a sports contest usually at a school or college.

1901 J. H. GRAY in W. B. Thomas *Athletics* v.103 The sack race was no longer a consolation race, for Mr. Thornton the *victor ludorum* is returned as the winner.

victrīx causa deīs placuit, sed victa Catōnī

∼ the victorious cause was pleasing to the gods, but the vanquished one to Cato.

LUCAN i.128. In the civil war with Caesar, Pompey was doomed, but at least his cause pleased the righteous—and infinitely self-righteous—Cato the Younger.

videō meliōra probōque, dēteriōra sequor

∼ I see the better course of action and I approve of it, but I follow the worse course.

OVID *Metamorphoses* vii.20. Medea realizes that she should not betray her father and help Jason, with whom she has fallen in love, to gain the Golden Fleece, but she cannot help herself.

vidē (abbreviated to vid. or v.)

~ see, refer to: a direction to the reader to refer to some other heading, passage, or work for fuller or further information.

First recorded use in English 1565.

1857 PHILLIP H. GOSSE *Omphalos* xii.354 (note) I have already proved that blood must have been in . . . the newly-created Man (*vide* p. 276, *supra*).

vidēlicet

~ that is to say, namely.

First recorded use in English 1464.

1602 T. FITZHERBERT *A defence of the Catholyke cause* 27 The words of our sauiour following the former in S. Mathew videlicet: I wil geeue thee the keyes of the kingdome of heauen.

vidē ut suprā

~ see what is given above.

See entries at VIDE *and* UT SUPRA.

vī et armīs

~ literally, 'with force and arms', violently, forcibly, by compulsion.

vincere scīs, Hannibal, victōriā ūtī nescīs

~ you know how to win, Hannibal, but you do not know how to use your victory.

LIVY xxii.li.4. After the Carthaginian Hannibal had inflicted upon the Romans the worst defeat they had ever known, at Cannae in 216 BC, Maharbal, the leader of his cavalry, begged him to send him ahead to Rome. If Hannibal did so, Maharbal told him, he would be dining on the Capitol three days later. Hannibal would not let him go, however, and earned this sad retort from his cavalry commander.

vincet amor patriae

~ love of the fatherland will prove supreme.

VIRGIL *Aeneid* vi.823. After the expulsion of King Tarquin, the sons of Brutus tried to bring him back to Rome. Brutus overcame his paternal love and had them executed. Virgil appears to view this with qualified approval. He says that Brutus was vastly in love with praise.

vincit quī sē vincit
~ he conquers who conquers himself.

An adaptation of PUBLILIUS SYRUS *Sententiae* B.21. The full maxim is: 'he conquers twice who conquers himself in victory.'

vīrēsque acquīrit eundō
~ she gathers strength as she goes.

VIRGIL *Aeneid* iv.175. Virgil here describes his terrifying personification of Rumour, who multiplies as she spreads.

virgō intācta
~ a woman of inviolate chastity.

1726 J. AYLIFFE *Parergon Juris Canonici Anglicani* 228 The wife of one Bury was divorc'd from him upon the Score of Frigidity, it appearing that for three years after the Marriage she remain'd *Virgo Intacta* on the Account of the Husband's Impotency.

virtūs post nummōs
~ virtue after money, i.e. money first.

HORACE *Epistles* I.i.54. The poet says that this is the general view—but not his.

vīta brevis, longa ars
~ life (is) short, art long.

A Latin translation of the Greek of Hippocrates, who compares the difficulties encountered in learning the art of medicine or healing with the shortness of human life. The proverb is now taken to refer not to medicine but to the durability of a work of art.

vīta nōn est vīvere sed valēre vīta est

See NON EST VIVERE SED VALERE VITA EST.

vīvāmus, mea Lesbia, atque amēmus
~ let us live, my Lesbia, and let us love.

CATULLUS v.1. Catullus asserts the supreme value of love when set against the everlasting night of extinction.

vīvat regīna!
~ long live the queen!

vīvat rēx!
~ long live the king!

vīvā vōce (abbreviated to **vīvā**)

∼ literally, 'by or with the living voice', i.e. spoken.

Used of an examination, etc., carried on or conducted by speech. First recorded use in English 1581.

1845 [PYCROFT] *Collegian's Guide* 265 In that case the *viva voce* examination and a second paper of questions may set all right.

vīvere est cōgitāre

∼ to live is to think.

CICERO *Tusculan Disputations* v.111. Cicero is here talking about the learned man.

vīvere mīlitāre est

∼ to live is to do one's military service.

SENECA *Letters* xcvi.5. Military service becomes a metaphor for human life.

vīvit post fūnera virtūs

∼ virtue lives beyond the grave.

vīxēre fortēs ante Agamemnona

∼ brave men lived before Agamemnon.

HORACE *Odes* IV.ix.25–6. Though heroes predated Agamemnon, they are not remembered because they had no Homer to sing of them. Horace insists on the power of poetry to confer immortality.

vīxit

∼ he/she has lived.

Inscribed on tombstones with the relevant number of years.

viz.

abbreviation of VIDELICET.

volentī nōn fit iniūria

∼ no injury is done to a willing person: a defence to an action whereby it is claimed that a person who sustained an injury agreed to risk such injury.

1658 E. WINGATE *Maximes of Reason* CXXII.482 If the Tenant in an Assise of an house desire the Plaintiffe to dine with him in the house, which the Plaintiffe doth accordingly, but doth not clame the house at that time; this is no entry or possession to cause the Assise to abate; because if he had been a stranger, he had been no trespasser for *volenti non fit injuria*.

vōx audīta perit, littera scrīpta manet

~ the heard word is lost, the written letter remains.

vōx et practereā nihil

~ literally, 'a voice and nothing besides', i.e. empty words.

Plutarch tells the story of a Spartan who plucked a nightingale and found so little substance that he exclaimed these words.

vōx faucibus haesit

~ his voice stuck in his throat.

VIRGIL *Aeneid* iv.280. Aeneas responds thus to Jupiter's rebuke, conveyed to him by Mercury, for frittering away his time in Carthage when he should be getting on to Italy and laying the foundations for the future of Rome.

vōx populī, vōx Deī

~ the voice of the people (is) the voice of God.

PETER OF BLOIS *Epistulae* 15.

zōnam perdidit
~ he has lost his money belt; he is in impoverished circumstances.

⇥ THE LATIN WRITERS ⇥

APULEIUS Lucius Apuleius (*fl.* AD 155).
Born at Madaura in Africa and educated at Carthage (where he later settled), Athens and Rome, he is famous for his *Metamorphoses* or *Golden Ass* (written in 160), a Latin novel in eleven books, the last of which reveals its philosophico-religious purpose.

AUGUSTINE Aurelius Augustinus, St Augustine of Hippo (AD 350–430).
Born in Roman Africa at Thagaste (Souk Ahras in Algeria), he was a passionate exponent of Christianity. The author of some ninety-three books as well as letters and sermons, he is best known for his *Confessions* (*c.*397–400) and *The City of God* (413–26).

AURELIUS Marcus Aurelius (AD 121–80).
Roman emperor from 161–80, his major literary achievement is his *Meditations*, a collection of Stoic aphorisms and reflections written in Greek over the last ten years of his reign while he was on campaign.

CAESAR Caius Julius Caesar (100–44 BC).
One of the great figures of the ancient world, both as a general and a statesman, he wrote *Commentaries*, comprising seven books (*De Bello Gallico*) on his campaign in Gaul and Britain (58–52 BC) and three (*De Bello Civili*) on the Civil War between himself and Pompey (49–48 BC). Cicero (*Brutus* 262) remarked that only a fool would try to improve on his accounts.

CATO Marcus Porcius Cato ('the Elder') (234–149 BC).
The only surviving work of this famously severe Roman statesman and moralist is *De Re Rustica* (On Farming).

CATULLUS Caius Valerius Catullus (*c.*84–*c.*54 BC).
Born in Verona, he wrote poetry on a number of themes but is most famous for his passionate love poems addressed to 'Les-

bia', who may have been a historical person (if so, probably the notorious aristocrat Clodia).

CICERO   Marcus Tullius Cicero (106–43 BC).
Born at Arpinum some seventy miles south-east of Rome, this celebrated Roman orator and statesman was a prolific writer on many themes. Among his fifty-eight surviving speeches are the six against Verres (*In Verrem*), the four against Catiline (*In Catilinam*), the sixteen *Philippics* against Mark Antony, and the speech in defence of Milo (*Pro Milone*). Two works on oratory are *De Oratore* (On the orator) and *Brutus*. We have more than 800 letters (including the collections *Ad Familiares* (To his friends) and *Ad Atticum* (To Atticus)). Among his philosophical works are the epistemological *Academica* (Academics), the political *De Republica* (On the Republic), *De Legibus* (On the Laws), the theological *De Natura Deorum* (On the Nature of the Gods), and the ethical *De Finibus* (On Ends), *Tusculanae Disputationes* (Tusculan Disputations), *De Senectute* (On Old Age) and *De Officiis* (On Duties). The *Rhetorica ad Herennium* (Treatise on Rhetoric) addressed to Herennius has been ascribed to Cicero but is not in fact by him.

CLAUDIAN   Claudius Claudianus (died *c.*AD 404).
Born in Alexandria in Egypt, and thus a native Greek-speaker, he turned to composing in Latin and became the last great Latin poet in the classical tradition. *The Rape of Persephone*, a poem in four books of which 1,100 lines survive, is today thought to be his finest work.

COLUMELLA   Lucius Junius Moderatus Columella (*fl.* AD 60).
Columella, who came from Gades (Cadiz) in Spain, composed a twelve-book treatise called *De Re Rustica* (On Farming) in about AD 60–65. This is written in prose except for book ten which is in hexameters.

ENNIUS   Quintus Ennius (239–169 BC).
Born at Rudiae in Calabria in south Italy, Ennius was a leading writer of Roman tragedy. His principal work was the *Annales* (Annals), a history of Rome from earliest times to his own in eighteen books of hexameter verse. Fewer than 600 lines of this survive. He reputedly wrote his own epitaph: 'Let no one

honour me with tears or attend my funeral with weeping. Why? I fly, still living, through the mouths of men.'

ERASMUS Desiderius Erasmus (AD 1466–1536).
Erasmus was a Dutch scholar and theologian who was Professor of Divinity at Cambridge from 1511 to 1513. A fine writer of Latin, in which language he wrote his *Moriae Encomium* (Praise of Folly) (1509), he launched modern biblical scholarship with his Greek New Testament. His *Adagia* (Adages), an anthology of more than 3,000 proverbs collected from the classical authors, was published in 1508 and established his reputation as the leading scholar of northern Europe.

FLORUS Lucius Annaeus Florus? (*fl.* AD 30–104).
Florus wrote the Latin history known as the *Epitome of all the Wars during Seven Hundred Years*, a two-book summary of Roman history up to the age of Augustus designed as a panegyric of the Roman people.

GELLIUS Aulus Gellius (*c.*AD 130–*c.*180).
Gellius wrote *Noctes Atticae* (Attic Nights) in twenty books, which have survived almost complete. A random collection of brief essays dealing with such topics as philosophy, history, law, grammar, and literary and textual criticism, it is especially valuable for the preservation of many passages from early Latin literature. It includes a number of good stories, that of Androclus and the lion among them.

HORACE Quintus Horatius Flaccus (65–8 BC).
Born the son of a freedman in Venusia (Venosa) in Apulia in south Italy, he later became part of the circle of Maecenas, the famous patron of the arts, and rubbed shoulders with the most powerful politicians and the leading poets of his day. His published works, all of which survive, consist of the *Epodes* and *Satires* (published in 30 BC), the *Epistles* (Epistulae)—of which the *Ars Poetica* (Art of Poetry) is the final one—and his major achievement, the *Carmina* (Odes) (published in 23 and 13 BC).

JEROME Eusebius Hieronymus, (St Jerome) (*c.*AD 347–420).
Born in a Christian family at Strido near Aquileia in north

Italy, he was the translator and editor of the Latin version of the Bible which we call the *Vulgate* (i.e. the 'common text').

JUSTINIAN Flavius Petrus Sabbatius Justinianus (*c*. AD 482–565).

Justinian, the Roman emperor at Constantinople from 527–565, rationalized and codified the Roman legal system. A team of codifiers assisted him to produce the *Corpus iuris civilis* (Complete Civil Law) which included the *Institutes*. Their greatest debt was to Ulpian (Domitius Ulpianus, died AD 223), one of the last of the leading Roman jurists, who wrote nearly 280 books.

JUVENAL Decimus Junius Juvenalis (*c*.AD 55–*c*.130).

Little is known about this celebrated satirical poet, who was born at Aquinum in Latium. His sixteen *Satires* were published in five books.

LABERIUS Decimus Laberius (*c*.105–43 BC).

This Roman knight was a distinguished writer of mimes (licentious farces).

LIVIUS ANDRONICUS Lucius Livius Andronicus (*c*.284–204 BC).

This Greek-speaking prisoner of war from Tarentum in south Italy translated Homer's *Odyssey* into Latin (only forty-six lines survive) and produced the first drama in Rome in 240. He is the father of Roman literature.

LIVY Titus Livius (59 BC–AD 17).

Born in Patavium (Padua) in north-east Italy, he became the friend of the emperor Augustus. His history of Rome from its foundation to 9 BC was in 142 books. Only 1–10 (dealing with 753–293 BC), 21–45 (dealing with 219–167 BC), and a fragment of 91 survive.

LUCAN Marcus Annaeus Lucanus (AD 39–65).

Born at Corduba (Cordoba) in Spain, he was educated at Rome. After joining a conspiracy against the emperor Nero, he was forced to commit suicide. His incomplete poem (ten books) on the *Bellum Civile* (civil war) deals with the war between Caesar and Pompey. Also known as *Pharsalia* after Caesar's victory over Pompey at Pharsalus in 48 BC, it espouses the republican cause—a bold stance under Nero.

LUCILIUS   Gaius Lucilius (*c*.108–102 BC).

This wealthy knight from Suessa Aurunca in Latium wrote thirty books of *Satires*, of which some 1,300 lines survive. He was the creator of the purely Roman form of satire.

LUCRETIUS   Titus Lucretius Carus (*c*.99–*c*.55 BC).

Lucretius' great philosophical poem *De Rerum Natura* (On Nature) communicates the teachings of the Greek philosopher Epicurus (341–270 BC) who was himself following in the footsteps of Democritus (460–*c*.357 BC). This didactic work aims to free men from a sense of guilt and the fear of death.

MANILIUS   Marcus Manilius (*fl*. at the start of the first century AD).

His apparently unfinished hexameter poem in five books entitled *Astronomica*, which sees design and 'heavenly reason' in the universe (*cf*. Lucretius), breaks off abruptly in the fifth book.

MARTIAL   Marcus Valerius Martialis (*c*.AD 40–103/4).

Born in Bilbilis in Spain, he came to Rome in 64 and retired to Bilbilis in 98 AD. His first known work is *De Spectaculis* (Of Spectacles), written to celebrate the opening of the Colosseum in Rome in AD 80. The twelve books of his satirical epigrams appeared between 86 and 101. Pliny speaks of him as 'talented, subtle, penetrating, witty, and sincere'.

NEPOS   Cornelius Nepos (*c*.100–*c*.25 BC).

A native of Cisalpine Gaul, he is remembered for his *De Viris Illustribus* (Lives of Famous Men), of which only one book out of at least sixteen survives. These lives are eulogizing and moralizing biographical sketches rather than historical biographies.

OVID   Publius Ovidius Naso (43 BC–AD 17).

Born at Sulmo in the Apennines about ninety miles east of Rome, he was educated at Rome and based there until in AD 8 he was somehow involved in an imperial scandal and banished by the emperor Augustus to Tomis (Costantza) on the Black Sea where he died. A prolific poet, he wrote *Amores* (Loves), *Heroides* (Heroines), *Ars Amatoria* (The Technique of Love), and *Remedia Amoris* (How to Fall out of Love) (1 AD). Decidedly more politically correct are *Fasti* (Calendar Days) and *Metamorphoses*, both begun in AD 2, the latter proving to be his masterpiece. Other works include the two great poems of his exile *Tristia* (Sad Poems) and *Epistulae ex Ponto* (Letters from the Black Sea). The cheerful immorality of much of his verse belies the fact that, alone of the Augustan poets, he was a respectable married man.

PERSIUS   Aulus Persius Flaccus (AD 34–62).
Born in an equestrian family at Volaterrae in Etruria, he fell under the influence of the Stoics at Rome. He wrote one book of six satires, modelled on Lucilius and Horace.

PETRONIUS ARBITER   (died AD 66).
Petronius pursued a successful political career and was admitted by the emperor Nero to his inner circle of intimates. He committed suicide after becoming involved in a conspiracy against the emperor. His vast picaresque novel, *Satyrica*, was in twenty or twenty-four books, of which only parts of books 14, 15, and 16 survive. The principal episode of the surviving fragments is the dinner-party flung by one of the most vivid characters in ancient literature, the *nouveau riche* Trimalchio.

PHAEDRUS   Gaius Julius Phaedrus (*c*.15 BC–*c*.AD 50).
A Thracian slave who became a freedman in the household of Augustus in Rome, he wrote a collection in verse of fables (*Fabulae Aesopiae*) in five books comprising some hundred stories. Serious or satirical in intent, they are based on the beast-stories of Aesop and other sources in the Aesopian tradition.

PLAUTUS   Titus Maccius Plautus (*c*.250–184 BC).
Born at Sarsina in Umbria, he was the writer of up to 130 comedies, twenty of which survive. The plays are all adapted from Greek originals.

PLINY the name of two Latin writers.

Gaius Plinius Secundus (AD 23/4–79), known as Pliny the Elder. An extraordinary polymath, he wrote the vast thirty-seven-book *Natural History*, which has survived. He was in command of the Roman fleet at Misenum when Mount Vesuvius erupted in AD 79 and died in a rescue mission to the disaster area.

Gaius Plinius Caecilius Secundus (AD 61/2–c.113), known as Pliny the Younger. Nephew and adopted son of Pliny the Elder, he had a highly successful political career which culminated in his admirable service as governor of Bithynia. His fame is due to his ten books of *Epistulae* (Letters). He delivered his speech in praise of the emperor Trajan (*Panegyricus*) when he became consul in AD 100.

PROPERTIUS Sextus Propertius (c.50 BC–after 16 BC).

Born at Asisium (Assisi) in Umbria, he was educated at Rome and became part of the circle of Maecenas, the great Augustan patron of the arts. He left four books of elegies, mainly love poems. His work is remarkable for its hypnotic intensity.

PUBLILIUS SYRUS (first century BC).

Brought to Rome, perhaps from Antioch, as a slave, he gained his freedom. He wrote a collection of moral maxims (*Sententiae*) for schools.

QUINTILIAN Marcus Fabius Quintillianus (born c.AD 35).

Born at Calagurris in Spain, Quintilian was a celebrated teacher of rhetoric at Rome. His most famous work is his *Institutio Oratoria* (Education of an Orator), published in twelve books in about AD 95.

SALLUST Gaius Sallustius Crispus (86–35 BC).

Born at Aminternum in the Sabine country north-east of Rome, he had a high-profile, if chequered political career. After being unsuccessfully prosecuted for extortion after his governorship of Numidia in 46 BC, he withdrew from public life and wrote the historical monographs, *Bellum Catilinae* (The War with Catiline), *Bellum Iugurthinum* (The War with Jugurtha), and the *Histories* of the years 78–67 BC. Of the *Histories* only fragments survive.

SENECA   Lucius Annaeus Seneca (*c*.4 BC–AD 65).
The son of the rhetoric teacher of the same name (born *c*.55 BC), whose *Controversiae* (Debates) and *Suasoriae* (Speeches of Advice) survive in part, Seneca the Younger became the tutor of the emperor Nero, but fell out of favour and was forced to commit suicide after being implicated in a conspiracy against the emperor. His profound Stoic beliefs sat ill with his fabulous wealth, since Stoicism places no value of worldly goods. Among other works, he wrote ten dialogues (*Dialogi*), including *De Ira* (Concerning Anger) and a collection of 124 *Letters to Lucilius* divided into twenty books. His most important poetical works are his nine tragedies adapted from Greek originals.

SILIUS ITALICUS   Tiberius Catius Asconius Silius Italicus (*c*.AD 26–101).
Born at Patavium (Padua), Silius pursued a successful political career. He wrote the longest surviving Latin poem *Punica* (The War with Carthage), an epic in seventeen books on the Second Punic War (218–201 BC).

STATIUS   Publius Papinius Statius (*c*.AD 45–*c*.96).
Statius was born at Naples, the son of a schoolmaster. His major work is the *Thebaid*, an epic in twelve books about the quarrel between Oedipus' sons Eteocles and Polyneices. The debt to Virgil's *Aeneid* is strong.

SUETONIUS   Gaius Suetonius Tranquillus (born *c*.AD 69).
He became a secretary at the imperial palace and thus had access to the imperial archives, but he was dismissed by Hadrian in 121/2, apparently for some indiscretion involving the emperor's wife. His surviving works include the *De Vita Caesarum* (Lives of the Caesars), comprising biographies of the first twelve emperors including Julius Caesar, and part of *De Viris Illustribus* (On Famous Men).

TACITUS   Publius (*or* Gaius) Cornelius Tacitus
(born AD 56 or 57, died after 117).
Possibly born in Narbonese Gual, Tacitus had a successful political career. His historical writings include his monograph about his father-in-law, *Agricola*, and his major works, the *Histories* (covering the years AD 69–96) and *Annals* (covering

the years AD 14–68). Much of these works is lost. Edward Gibbon thought more highly of Tacitus than of any other ancient historian.

TERENCE   Publius Terentius Afer (died 159 BC?).
An ex-slave from Carthage, Terence wrote six comedies adapted from the Greek.

TERTULLIAN   Florens Quintus Septimius Tertullianus (c.AD 160–225).
Born in Carthage and brought up as a pagan, Tertullian was converted to Christianity before 197. He was the father of Latin Christian theology. Among his works are his *Apologeticum* (Speech for the Defence) in which he aims to secure protection for Christians.

TIBULLUS   Albius Tibullus (c.55–19 BC).
A friend of Horace and Ovid, Tibullus wrote two books of elegies. His favoured themes are love and country life.

VALERIUS FLACCUS   Gaius Valerius Flaccus (d. AD 92 or 93).
He wrote an incomplete epic poem, *Argonautica* (the story of Jason and the Golden Fleece), which breaks off abruptly in the eighth book.

VARRO   Marcus Terentius Varro (116–27 BC).
Born at Reate in Sabine territory, Varro was Rome's outstanding antiquarian and philologist. We know the titles of fifty-five of his works but only two of them survive in more than fragmentary form. These are books 5–10 of *De Lingua Latina* (On the Latin Language), dedicated to Cicero, and the three books of *De Re Rustica* (On Farming).

VEGETIUS   Flavius Vegetius Renatus
A military writer under the emperor Theodosius (AD 383–95). His *Epitoma Rei Militaris* (Military Epitome) in four books is the sole account of Roman military practice which has survived intact.

VIRGIL   Publius Vergilius Maro (70–19 BC).
Born at Mantua in Cisalpine Gaul, Virgil was educated at Cre-

mona, Milan, and Rome. He became part of the circle of Mae-cenas, the great Augustan patron, and a friend and supporter of Augustus. His pastoral poems, the *Eclogues*, were perhaps published in 37 BC, the *Georgics*, his four-book didactic poem on farming, in 29 BC, and his great twelve-book epic, the *Aeneid*, posthumously. He was buried near Naples. Dante regarded Virgil as *il nostro maggior poeta* (our greatest poet).

VITRUVIUS Vitruvius Pollio (*fl.* 50 BC).

Vitruvius was an engineer and architect of the first century BC. His treatise in ten books *De Architectura* (On Architecture) is dedicated to the emperor Augustus.

VULGATE *see under* JEROME.

❧ GENERAL INDEX ❧

Arranged by topics. There are separate **indexes for Christianity and the Church**, **The Law**, and **Proverbs**.
 Entries of not more than four words are given complete. Longer entries are given with up to four words followed by three dots.

Appearances

cucullus non facit monachum
esse quam videri
facies non omnibus una
fronti nulla fides
in cauda venenum
ne fronti crede
nimium ne crede colori
prima facie

Architecture

in antis
opus alexandrinum
opus reticulatum
opus sectile

Argument

advocatus diaboli
argumentum ad verecundiam
Athanasius contra mundum
audi alteram partem
contra mundum
e contrario
obscurum per obscurius
per contra
pro [and] contra
reductio ad absurdum

Art (*see also* **Painting**, *etc.*)

ars est celare artem
ars gratia artis
ars longa, vita brevis
honos alit artes
magnum opus
opus artificem probat

Astronomy

Georgium sidus
primum mobile
Via Lactea

Beauty

decus et tutamen
matre pulchra filia pulchrior
o matre pulchra filia . . .
simplex munditiis
spretaeque iniuria formae

Beginnings and endings

ab aeterno
ab initio
ab origine
ab ovo
ab ovo usque . . .
ab urbe condita
ad finem
dabit deus his quoque . . .
de integro
exitus acta probat
finem lauda
finem respice
finis
finis coronat opus
fons et origo
fuimus Troes
fuit Ilium
imprimis
incipit
in limine
in ovo
in statu nascendi
nascentes morimur
obsta principiis
omne vivum ex ovo
respice finem
terminus ad quem
terminus a quo

Behaviour

o tempora! o mores!

Belief and unbelief
credat Iudaeus
Apella, . . .
fere libenter
homines id . . .
incredulus odi

Betrayal (*see* **Trust
and treachery**)

Bible (*see also
separate index on*
**Christianity and
the Church**)
apage Satanas
consummatum est
crescite et
multiplicamini
ecce homo!
fiat lux
Iesus Nazarenus Rex
Iudaeorum
noli me tangere
radix malorum est
cupiditas
retro me, satana . . .

Blessings
annuit coeptis
auditque vocatus
Apollo
benigno numine

Biography
apologia pro vita sua
curriculum vitae
de te fabula narratur
floruit

Body
a capite ad calcem

corpus vile
fiat experimentum
in corpore . . .
in utero
membrum virile
mons Veneris
nemo liber est qui . . .
situs inversus

Books (in general)
editio princeps
ex libris
habent sua fata
libelli
helluo librorum
imprimatur
literati
quicquid agunt
homines . . .
vade mecum
variorum

**Books (finding your
way about them)**
addendum
ad locum
ante
cetera desunt
confer (cf.)
corrigenda
desunt cetera
et al.
et cetera (etc)
et sic de ceteris
et sic de similibus
exempli gratia (e.g.)
ibidem (ibid., ib.)
id est (i.e.)
incipit
index librorum
prohibitorum

infra
in re
loco citato (loc. cit.)
nota bene (NB)
opere citato (op. cit.)
passim
quod vide (q.v.)
re
recto
scilicet (sc.)
seq.
stet
supra
ut supra
verso
vide (vid., v.)
videlicet (viz.)
vide ut supra

Can and can't
licet
ne plus ultra
nihil obsat
non licet
non licet omnibus
adire . . .
non omnia possunt
omnes
non placet
pace tua
placet
pleno iure
possunt quia posse
videntur

Censorship
ad usum Delphini
index expurgatorius
index librorum
prohibitorum
in usum Delphini

Certainty and doubt

ad praesens ova . . .
alea iacta est
Athanasius contra mundum
cum grano salis
ex cathedra
in dubio
in nubibus
lupum auribus tenere
non liquet

Character

abeunt studia in mores
ab uno disce omnes
eiusdem farinae
ex ungue leonem
ex uno disce omnes
miles gloriosus
patris est filius
suaviter in modo, fortiter . . .

Change and transience

mutatis mutandis
mutato nomine
omnia mutantur, . . .
tempora mutantur, . . .

Choice

aut Caesar aut nullus
de duobus malis . . .
incidis in Scyllam . . .

Christianity and the Church (*see separate Index*)

Compromise

flecti, non frangi

Conquest (*see Victory and defeat*)

Cooperation

inter nos
inter se
manus manum lavat
modus vivendi
nemine contradicente
nemine dissentiente
posse
quorum

Country and Town

beatus ille qui . . .
magna civitas, magna solitudo
o fortunatos nimium . . .
rus in urbe

Courage

ad utrumque paratus
audaces fortuna iuvat
audentes fortuna iuvat
aude sapere
fortes fortuna adiuvat
fortiter in re . . .
ignis aurum probat . . .

inest clementia forti
in utrumque paratus
ne cede malis
tu ne cede malis . . .

Crime and punishment

deprendi miserum est
flagrante delicto
ille crucem sceleris pretium . . .
locus delicti
mea culpa
quid pro quo

Critics and criticism

apparatus criticus
crux (criticorum)
damnant quod non intellegunt
locus desperatus
ne sutor ultra crepidam
sutor ne supra crepidam . . .

Custom

ex more
more maiorum

Danger

anguis in herba
auribus teneo lupum
cave
caveat
cavendo tutus
graviora manent
Hannibal ad portas
latet anguis in herba

adsum
aegrotat
alma mater
alumnus
artium baccalaureus
    (BA)
artium magister
    (MA)
emeritus
exeat
floreat Etona
honoris causa
in statu pupillari
literae humaniores
literati
Magister Artium
    (MA)
magna cum laude
non scholae sed
    vitae . . .
schola cantorum
summa cum laude

Emotion and the lack of it

ab imo pectore
absit invidia
aequo animo
caeca invidia est
inest clementia forti
sine ira et studio
taedium vitae

Enemies

fas est et . . .
Iuppiter hostis
occultae inimicitiae
    magis
    timendae . . .
versus (ver., vs. v.)

Epitaphs

beatae memoriae
hic iacet
in memoriam
memoria in aeterna
nihil quod tetigit
    non . . .
nullum quod
    tetigit . . .
obiit
pro memoria
si monumentum
    requiris,
    circumspice
siste, viator
ubi saeva
    indignatio . . .
vixit

Equality and inequality

cedo maiori
ceteris paribus
da locum melioribus
impar congressus
    Achilli
inter pares
non passibus aequis
pari passu
prima inter pares
primus inter pares
proxime accessit

Eternity

ad infinitum
in aeternum
in infintum
in perpetuum
in saecula
    saeculorum

sub specie
    aeternitatis

Exile

aqua et igne
    interdictus

Experience

eventus stultorum
    magister
experientia docet
    stultos
experto crede
expertus metuit
non ignara mali . . .
quorum pars magna
    fui

Fame and obscurity

clarum et venerabile
    nomen
digito monstrari et
    dicier . . .
fama semper vivat!
filius nullius
sic itur ad astra

Family

domus et placens
    uxor
filius nullius
in loco parentis
materfamilias
optimis parentibus
par nobile fratrum
patris est filius

Fast and slow

crescit eundo
cunctando restituit
    rem
festina lente

Fate

desine fata deum
    flecti . . .
dira Necessias
ducunt volentem
    fata
fata obstant
fata viam invenient
sic erat in fatis

Fear

ante tubam trepidat
degeneres animos
    timor arguit
expertus metuit
horresco referens
horror vacui
hunc tu caveto
in terrorem

Fire

alere flammam
ignis fatuus

Flowers

laus tibi

Food and drink (*see also* **Wine**)

ab ovo usque ad
    mala
esse oportet ut
    vivas, . . .
magnum bonum
non ut edam vivo . . .
panem et circenses
sero venientibus
    ossa
ubi mel, ibi apes

Fortune

faber est quisque
    fortunae . . .
fortuna vitrea est . . .
stet fortuna domus

Friendship

alter ego
alter idem
alter ipse amicus
amici probantur
    rebus adversis
amicus certus . . .
amicus usque ad
    aras
Arcades ambo
donec eris sospes, . . .
felicitas multos
    habet amicos
fidus Achates
idem velle . . .

Future

in futuro
quid sit futurum
    cras . . .

Genius

nullum magnum
    ingenium sine . . .

Gifts and giving

acceptissima semper
    munera sunt, . . .
auctor pretiosa facit
beneficium
    accipere . . .
bis dat qui cito dat
data et accepta
ex gratia
timeo Danaos . . .

God and gods (*see also separate index on* **Christianity and the Church**)

a Deo et rege
ad maiorem Dei
    gloriam
Dei gratia
Deo adiuvante
Deo favente
Deo gratias
Deo volente (DV)
deus absconditus
Deus vobiscum!
Deus vult
dis aliter visum est
Domine, dirige nos
Dominus vobiscum
Dominus
    illuminatio mea
est deus in nobis
Iuppiter hostis
Iuppiter pluvius
Iuppiter tonans
iure divino
lares et penates
laus Deo
magna mater
penates
permitte dis cetera
si dis placet
tantaene animis
    caelestibus irae?
vera incessu patuit
    dea
vox populi, vox Dei

Good and evil

Acherontis pabulum
bona fide

Honour and dishonour

ab honesto virum bonum . . .
a cuspide corona
avito viret honore
casta est quam nemo . . .
falsus in uno, . . .
fidem qui perdit, . . .
homo antiqua virtute . . .
honor vitutis praemium
honos alit artes
infra dignitatem (infra dig.)

Hope and despair

at spes non fracta
dum spiro, spero
inter spem et metum
magnae spes altera Romae
nil desperandum
spero meliora
una salus victis . . .

Humour (see Laughter)

Human Race

di nos quasi pilas . . .
errare humanum est
hominis est errare
homo est sociale animal
homo homini lupus
homo sum . . .
humanum est errare

proprium humani ingenii est . . .
theatrum mundi

Ignorance

argumentum ad ignorantiam
ignorantia legis neminem excusat
ignoti nulla cupido
ignotum per ignotius
ne Aesopum quidem trivit
omne ignotum pro magnifico
pons asinorum

In and out

ab extra
ab intra
intra muros

Important and unimportant

de asini umbra disceptare
filius terrae
in capite

Insults

Acherontis pabulum
spretaeque iniuria formae

Joy and sorrow (see also Happiness)

amari aliquid
annus horribilis
da dextram misero
est quaedam flere voluptas

felix culpa
hinc illae lacrimae
infandum, regina, iubes renovare . . .
iucundi acti labores
lacrimae rerum
leve fit, quod bene . . .
medio de fonte leporum . . .
multis ille bonis flebilis . . .
post equitem sedet atra . . .
recepto dulce mihi furere . . .
sunt lacrimae rerum

Justice, the just and the unjust

et sceleratis sol oritur
fia iustitia et pereat mundus
fiat iustitia et ruant coeli
iudex damnatur ubi nocens absolvitur
ius suum cuique
iustitia omnibus
ruat coelum

Kings and queens

a Deo et rege
aut regem aut fatuum nasci . . .
Caesar non supra grammaticos
ego et rex meus
fidei defensor
interrex

vivere est cogitare
vivere militare est

Light and dark
clarior e tenebris
fiat lux
hinc lucem et
  pocula . . .
lumen naturale
lumen siccum

Like and unlike
Davus sum, non
  Oedipus
eiusdem farinae
eiusdem generis
et hoc (or id) genus
  omne
hoc genus omne
id genus omne
impar congressus
  Achilli
instar omnium
noscitur e sociis
patris est filius
pari passu
prima inter pares
primus inter pares
quantum mutatus
  abillo
rara avis
sui generis
tu quoque

Literature
grammatici certant
literae humaniores
literati
littera scripta manet
locus classicus
persona

Logic
ad absurdum
a fortiori
a posteriori
a priori
causa sine qua non
certum est quia
  impossibile . . .
conditio sine qua
  non
credo quia
  absurdum/impos-
  sibile . . .
eo ipso
ergo
exceptis excipiendis
ex hypothesi
ex pede Heculem
hypotheses non
  fingo
ipso facto
mutatis mutandis
petitio principii
post hoc, ergo
  propter . . .
rebus sic stantibus
sensu lato
sensu stricto

Love and lovers
agnosco veteris
  vestigia flammae
amantes amentes
amantium irae
  amoris
  integratio . . .
amare et sapere . . .
casta est quam
  nemo . . .
credula res amor est

improbe Amor, quid
  non . . .
militat omnis amans
odi et amo
omnia vincit amor,
  et . . .
quis fallere possit
  amantem?
si vis amari, ama
trahit sua quemque
  voluptas
traicit et fati
  litora . . .

Madness and sanity
amabilis insania
amantes amentes
aut insanit homo
  aut . . .
compos mentis
insanus omnis
  furere credit . . .
non compos mentis
quem Jupiter vult
  perdere . . .
quicquid delirant
  reges . . .
semel insanivimus
  omnes

Many and few
numerus clausus
ohe! iam satis

Medicine
in vitro
in vivo
locum tenens
sal volatile
similia similibus
  curantur

Meeting and parting

ave atque vale
ave, Caesar, morituri te . . .
insalutato hospite
morituri te salutamus
salve
vale

Memory

aliquid haeret
beatae memoriae
forsan et haec olim . . .
in memoriam
lapsus memoriae
memorabilia
memoria in aeterna
memoriter
mendacem memorem esse oportet
pro memoria

Men

ad hominem
argumentum ad hominem
arma virumque cano
caelebs quid agam
expende Hannibalem
homo nullius coloris
iure humano
lupus est homo homini
novus homo
posse
quorum

quot homines tot sententiae

Men and women

nec tecum possum vivere . . .
Paete, non dolet

Middle

in medias res
in medio tutissimus ibis
mediocria firma
medio tutissimus ibis
medium tenuere beati
via media

Mind

mens agitat molem
mens rea
mens sana in corpore . . .
mens sibi conscia recti
o miseras hominum mentes . . .

Mistakes

errare humanum est
hominis est errare
humanum est errare

Moderation

aurea mediocritas
est modus in rebus
in medio tutissimus ibis
mediocria firma
medio tutissimus ibis

medium tenuere beati
ne nimium
ne quid nimis
quantum sufficit
satis

Money

ad crumenam
alieni appetens, sui profusus
amor nummi
argumentum ad crumenam
auri sacra fames
LSD
lucri bonus est odor . . .
non olet
per annum
per caput
per centum
pro forma
pro rata
quantum meruit
quietus
radit usque ad cutem
radix malorum est cupiditas
uti foro
virtus post nummos

Motion

mobile perpetuum
perpetuum mobile
viresque acquirit eundo

Pain (*see under* **Pleasure and pain**)

Painting, drawing, engraving, and sculpture
deciens repetita placebit
ecce homo!
fecit
insculpsit
Mater Dolorosa
noli me tangere
pictor ignotus
pinxit
sculpsit
ut pictura poesis

Past
consule Planco
laudator temporis acti
non sum qualis eram . . .
olim
quondam
status quo ante (bellum)

Patriotism
amor patriae
ducit amor patriae
dulce et decorum est . . .
pro aris et focis
pro patria
vincet amor patriae

Peace
candida Pax
cedant arma togae

pax
pax vobis(cum)!
si vis pacem, . . .
ubi solitudinem faciunt . . .
solitudinem faciunt, pacem appellant

People
aura popularis
belua multorum capitum
coram populo
faex populi
miserabile vulgus
mobile vulgus
odi profanum vulgus . . .
panem et circenses
populus vult decipi, ergo . . .
pro bono publico
profanum vulgus
referendum
salus populi suprema lex . . .
vox populi, vox Dei

Perfection
ad unguem

Philosophy
a posse ad esse
cogito, ergo sum
de nihilo nihilum, . . .
ex nihilo nihil fit
gigni de nihilo nihilum, . . .
in esse
in posse

in potentia
nil igitur mors est . . .
nunc stans
qua
sartor resartus
summum bonum

Places
alibi
Campus Martius
delenda est Carthago
dum Roma deliberat, Saguntum . . .
esto perpetua
ex Africa semper aliquid . . .
facilis descensus Averni
Gallia est omnis divisa . . .
genius loci
in distans
in loco
in situ
in vacuo
locus delicti
locus in quo
locus sigilli
longo intervallo
non licet omnibus adire . . .
Troia fuit
ubi bene, ibi patria
ubi mel, ibi apes
ultima Thule

Pleasure and pain
a bene placito
ad arbitrium
ad libitum (ad lib.)

probatum est
quod erat
  demonstrandum
  (QED)
solvitur ambulando

Proverbs (*see separate index*)

Race
credat ludaeus
  Apella, . . .
furor Teutonicus
Graeculus esuriens
non Angli, sed angeli
perfervidum
  ingenium
  Scotorum
Punica fides
timeo Danaos et
  dona . . .

Rage
furor arma ministrat
furor Teutonicus
ira furor brevis est
tantaene animis
  caelestibus irae?

Reading (*see also Books*)
helluo liborum
lector benevole
tolle lege, tolle lege

Reality
bona fide
de facto
esse quam videri
in esse

Relevance
ad rem

Religion (*see also separate index on* **Christianity and the Church**)
absit omen
astra castra, numen
  lumen
bonis avibus
malis avibus
procul, o procul
  este, . . .
religio laici
religio loci
santum sanctorum
tantum religio
  potuit suadere . . .

Repetition
crambe repetita
ecce iterum
  Crispinus

Revenge
exoriare aliquis
  nostris ex . . .
inhumanum
  verbum est ultio
lex talionis
mortui non mordent
nemo me impune
  lacessit
quid pro quo

Reversal
vice versa

Rome and Romans
ab urbe condita
  (AUC)

anno urbis conditae
civis Romanus sum
gens togata
o fortunatam
  natam . . .
panem et circenses
quid Romae faciam?
Roma locuta est . . .
Senatus Populusque
  Romanus (SPQR)
tantae molis erat
  Romanam . . .
ultimus
  Romanorum
urbem latericiam
  invenit, . . .
urbi et orbi
utinam unam
  cervicem haberet!

Same and different
Davus sum, non
  Oedipus
inter alia
inter alios
non passibus aequis
quantum mutatus
  ab illo

School slang
cave
pax

Science
aqua regia
aqua vitae
concordia discors
sensu lato
sensu stricto

Style (in writing)

callida iunctura
curiosa felicitas
olet lucerna
parturiunt montes,
   nascetur
   ridiculus ...
redolet lucerna
sesquipedalia verba

Success and failure

annus mirabilis
asinus ad lyram
aut non tentaris aut
   perfice

Suffering

Ilias malorum
optimum est pati
   quod ...
perfer, obdura
per varios casus,
   per ...
quicquid delirant
   reges
   plectuntur ...
quousque tandem
   abutere,
   Catilina ...

Taste

arbiter elegantiae/
   elegantiarum
de gustibus non
   est ...
emunctae naris

Teaching and learning

docendo discimus
fas est et ...

longum iter est
   per ...
quae nocent docent
qui docet discit
sit non doctissima
   coniunx
sus Minervam

Thinking

cogito, ergo sum
in pectore
vivere est cogitare

Threats

brutum fulmen
fulmen brutum

Time (*see also* Past, Present, Future, Eternity, and Transience)

ad extremum
ad interim
ad Kalendas Graecas
aetatis suae
anno aetatis suae
Anno Domini
anno hegirae
anno mundi
anno urbis conditae
ante-bellum
ante meridiem (a.m.)
circa (c., ca.)
de die in diem
diem perdidi
e vestigio
horas non numero
   nisi ...
in statu quo ante
labuntur et
   imputantur

per diem
per mensem
post factum
post meridiem (p.m.)
potius sero quam
   nunquam
pro hac vice
pro tempore (pro
   tem.)
tempus, edax rerum

Town (*see* Country and town)

Transience

dum loquor, hora
   fugit
eheu! fugaces
   labuntur anni
fugit hora
fugit irreparabile
   tempus
hora fugit
omnia mutantur,
   nos et ...
sic transit gloria
   mundi
tempora mutantur,
   nos et ...
tempus, edax rerum
tempus fugit
ubi sunt?

Travel

caelum non
   animum
   mutant ...
in transitu
vade mecum

Trial and error

alia tentanda via est

CHRISTIANITY AND THE CHURCH

a cruce salus
adeste fideles
ad limina (Apostolorum)
ad maiorem Dei gloriam
Agnus Dei
anathema sit
anima naturaliter Christiana
ave Maria

Corpus Christi

de profundis
Dies Irae

fidei defensor
filioque

gloria

habemus Papam

in nomine Patris . . .
in partibus infidelium
ite, missa est
iubilate Deo

Kyrie eleison

locum tenens
locus poenitentiae
lux mundi

magnificat

Mater Dolorosa
mea culpa
miserere
Missa solemnis

nisi Dominus, frustra
non nobis, Domine
nunc dimittis

opus Dei

Pater Noster
propaganda fide

quicunque vult (salvus esse)
quo vadis (,domine)?

religio laici
resurgam

sancta simplicitas
scala Caeli
sic transit gloria mundi
Stabat Mater (dolorosa)
sursum corda

urbi et orbi

vade retro me, satana
veni Creator Spiritus
Via Crucis
Via Dolorosa

⚒ INDEX ON THE LAW ⚒

In classical Latin there was no letter 'j'. This dictionary has followed Latin usage in printing consonantal 'i' (pronounced 'y'), and so, if you wish to track down a Latin word beginning with 'j', you should look under 'i'.

status quo
status quo ante (bellum)
sub iudice
sub lite
sub poena
sub rosa
suggestio falsi
sui iuris

suppressio veri
tertius gaudens
ultima ratio
ultra vires
uti possidetis
versus (ver., vs., v.)
volenti non fit iniuria

⇒ INDEX OF PROVERBS ⇒

These proverbs can be found in the dictionary in their Latin equivants.

better late than never | potius sero quam nunquam

a bird in the hand is worth two in the bush | ad praesens ova cras pullis sunt meliora

between the devil and the deep blue sea | a fronte praecipitium, a tergo lupi; inter canem et lupum

birds of a feather flock together | pares cum paribus facillime congregantur

blood from a stone | ab asino lanam; aquam e pumice nunc postulas

to carry coals to Newcastle | Alcinoo poma dare; crocum in Ciliciam ferre; noctuas Athenas ferre

every man to his taste / sua cuique voluptas

example is better that precept | longum iter est per praecepta, breve et efficax per exempla

familiarity breeds contempt | maior e longinquo reverentia

forewarned is forearmed | praemonitus, praemunitus

the game is not worth the candle | aureo hamo piscari

I'll scratch your back if you scratch mine | manus manum lavat

kill two birds with one stone | uno saltu duos apros capere *the leopard does not change its spots* | lupus pilum mutat, non mentem

let the cobbler stick to his last | ne sutor ultra crepidam

let sleeping dogs lie | quieta non movere

moderation in all things | est modus in rebus

necessity is the mother of invention | magister artis ingeniique largitor venter

out of sight, out of mind | absens haeres non erit

out of the frying pan into the fire | incidis in Scyllam cupiens vitare Charybdim

pearls before swine | margaritas ante porcos

still waters run deep | altissima quaeque flumina minimo sono labi

strike while the iron is hot | occasionem cognosce

talk of the devil | lupus in fabula

teach one's grandmother to suck eggs | sus Minervam

there's many a slip twixt cup and lip | inter caesa et porrecta

there's no accounting for tastes | de gustibus non est disputandum

there's no smoke without fire | flamma fumo est proxima

virtue is its own reward | ipsa quidem pretium virtus sibi

while there's life there's hope | dum spiro, spero

you have hit the nail on the head | rem acu tetigisti